Crochet
200 Q&A

Crochet
200 Q&A

Questions answered on everything from basic
stitches to finishing touches

Rita Taylor

BARRON'S

A Quantum Book

Copyright © 2009 Quantum Publishing

First edition for North America and the Philippines published in 2009 by
Barron's Educational Series, Inc.

All inquiries should be addressed to:
Barron's Educational Series, Inc.
250 Wireless Boulevard
Hauppauge, New York 11788
www.barronseduc.com

ISBN-13: 978-0-7641-6258-9
ISBN-10: 0-7641-6258-6

Library of Congress Control Number: 2009920839

This book is published and produced by
Quantum Books
6 Blundell Street
London N7 9BH

QUMC2Q2

Publisher: Anastasia Cavouras
Editor: Sarah Burnside
Editorial Assistant: Samantha Warrington
Production: Rohana Yusof
Photographer: John Gaffen
Design: EnvyDesign Ltd.

Printed in China by Midas Printing International Ltd.
9 8 7 6 5 4 3 2 1

All images are the copyright of Quantum Publishing, except for the photo on page 202,
which is courtesy of Carol Ventura (www.tapestrycrochet.com).

CONTENTS

INTRODUCTION

The history of crochet is obscured by myths. It is claimed by some that it was invented by shepherds, who used a miniature version of their crook to turn the sheeps' wool into rugs. Others suggest that it was developed by sailors, who were used to manipulating ropes to make nets. It may have been used as early as the thirteenth century to decorate church vestments, but the precise dates of these pieces are not known. The simplicity of the tool and method of working suggest that it could have been one of the earliest forms of "cloth" making. Like all fiber-related crafts, the products deteriorate quickly, leaving no hard evidence. The only pieces still in existence date from the nineteenth century. These early pieces have a similar appearance to needle-made laces and were probably an attempt to copy them using a quicker and less expensive form of needlework. There were no written patterns. Crochet workers kept a series of samples, of needle lace and of crochet, mounted into an exercise book from which they could work.

It is also possible that crochet developed from a form of embroidery known as tambour work. In this craft, a fine hook was used to draw thread through a piece of fabric stretched across a wooden hoop. It made a stitch similar to a chain stitch in embroidery. It is not known when someone decided that the background fabric could be discarded and the chain stitches worked "in the air". From here it was an obvious move to make other stitches into the open chains. These stitches became more and more elaborate, and patterns were devised that were not based on needle laces.

Most of the pieces of crochet that have survived are examples of Irish crochet, a form which flourished in Ireland during the potato famine of the mid-1840s. This type of crochet was introduced by nuns who had learned the technique in the convents of France, perhaps giving some credence to the story that it began much earlier in the religious houses of Europe. The motifs were based on those found in guipure lace. Being small and portable, they could be made by several women in the community who would then link them together with a background mesh to form beautifully intricate household linen or special occasion garments. This form of crochet became very popular and commanded a high price, bringing much-needed income to the villages.

As the population grew, so did the market for crochet, and with it came a demand for patterns. In England, crochet was taught in schools, and several members of the Royal family sponsored schools specifically for different types of needlework, including crochet. This all generated further interest and stimulated the publication of numerous books in the late nineteenth century. *Weldon's Practical Crochet* and *Godey's Lady's Book* contained patterns for all kinds of articles from "babies first drawers" to antimacassars and bedspreads. Different forms of crochet were devised using other tools such as hairpins, broomsticks and Tunisian hooks. Patterns were written for articles you would never think you needed, such as hair tidies and jam jar covers, even for skirts to cover the legs of the piano stool!

This propensity to cover every available surface with crochet may have contributed to its decline in popularity following its heyday in the Victorian and Edwardian eras. However, in the 1920s interest increased again with the publication of patterns for the loose tops and jackets fashionable after the First World War. The reverse trend for tight-fitting knitwear ousted it once more in the 1930s and 40s, until its next heyday in the 1960s. Again it was the shape of the tops, short and straight, that helped to bring about this popularity. Once it caught on, shapes and styles of all kinds were seen everywhere, particularly the loosely crocheted minidresses a la Mary Quant. The fashion continued on into the 1970s, with the younger generation particularly wearing vests and jackets made out of brightly colored granny squares. The other stimulus to this trend may have been the availability of new yarns. Up until then, crochet had usually been carried out in fine cotton or linen thread but the advent of a wider variety of fibers in various thicknesses helped to increase its use for clothing.

We now have an even greater choice of fibers, and it seems that crochet is having another wave of popularity. In writing this book I hope to stimulate those who have not yet tried the craft and those who are already keen crocheters and who would like to progress further. I have tried to demystify the language of crochet and to pass on some of the techniques that I have learned from studying samples and working from patterns from all eras. I hope that it will help to prolong the interest in a simple but beautiful craft.

1

TOOLS AND MATERIALS

Your hook and yarn are the most important tools when it comes to starting crochet, but there are a number of other pieces of equipment that are useful.

Question 1:
What is crochet?

The term "crochet" is applied to both the fabric and the means of making that fabric with a hooked implement and a single thread or fiber. The name "crochet" comes from the French word "croc," or possibly the Norse word "kroke," meaning hook.

The craft's true age is often disputed. There are claims that it began in the Stone Age, while others say that it originated in China and some that it was practiced among Arabic civilizations. However, since no pieces of identifiable crochet from these early times have yet been found, its origins are still a mystery.

However, there are pieces of crochet still in existence that date back from the 16th century. These pieces of crochet were used to trim church linen and other ecclesiastical items as an alternative to the more expensive bobbin and needle-made laces. For this reason, it was often referred to as "Nun's Work," or "Nun's Lace."

The craft was subsequently taken to Ireland, probably by French nuns, in the 18th century. It was intended that the local women should make pieces of crochet that they could then sell in order to alleviate some of the poverty brought on by the famine. Much of the beautiful work that they created was displayed at the Great Exhibition in 1851 and may have played a part in increasing its popularity elsewhere.

LEFT Antique doll from the 1950s wearing a hand-crocheted dress.

Question 2:
What is the difference between knitting and crochet?

Crochet differs from knitting in that it uses only one tool. This tool has a hook at one end, while knitting needles are straight and pointed.

In most forms of crochet, only one loop or stitch is kept on the needle at any one time before the next movement is made, while knitting creates stitch after stitch held in a row on the needle. These stitches are all live; they cannot be taken off the needle without unraveling back to the beginning. Crochet stitches, however, are interlocked and able to stand alone, free of any tool. Each stitch is only attached to those immediately adjacent to it, horizontally rather than vertically. If a stitch is snagged or broken, it will not unravel the stitches above and below it. Crochet also has the advantage that it can be easily tried on or measured as the stitches are not held on a needle or any other tool, unlike knitting, where the live stitches have to be kept on a stitch holder of some kind. It is also easier to see your mistakes in crochet, which can then be fixed immediately.

BELOW LEFT Crochet hook and colorful piece of work in progress.

BELOW RIGHT Knitting needles with live stitches on the needle.

Question 3:
What can I make with crochet?

As well as using crochet for trims and edgings on household linens of all kinds, from handkerchiefs to bedding, it can also be used to make complete items such as tablecloths, doilies, cushion covers and curtains. Single-strand, or multistrand yarn can be crocheted into warm afghans or floor rugs, and string or twine can be used to create shopping bags or even nets to cover your fruit and vegetables in the garden.

Leather thronging or raffia can be turned into sturdy baskets or ornamental items, such as covered lamp bases and pot covers. Torn fabric strips can be crocheted into attractive and washable mats that are easy and economical to make using only the basic stitches.

Whatever you can make with knitting, you can make more quickly with crochet: hats, gloves, scarves and even socks or slippers as well as the usual sweaters and jackets for adults and children and fine lacy dresses and shawls for babies. There is no limit to what you can make once you give your imagination free rein. The more you experiment, the more you will discover what you can do.

BELOW Depending on the yarn you choose, crochet can be used for almost anything.

Question 4:
Is there more than one type of crochet?

There are a number of types, many of which evolved through the idea that other forms of lace could be made more quickly and economically. Perhaps Irish crochet is the most well-known in this respect, where the designs were derived from Venetian lace.

I here are also two types based on a square background. Filet crochet developed from needle lace, which has a design darned onto a square mesh. Surface crochet is reminiscent of cross-stitch or similar counted thread embroidery work, where the design is created on top of a piece of single crochet after it is finished.

Other forms of crochet are hairpin and broomstick, which both require other tools in addition to the crochet hook. Hairpin crochet makes strips that need to be joined together, broomstick makes a very loose and open form of crochet. Finally there is Tunisian crochet, also known as tricot or Afghan crochet. This is a cross between knitting and crochet, worked with a longer hook to accommodate a number of stitches on alternate rows.

Other forms of crochet you may hear mentioned – jacquard, beaded and patchwork – are merely variations on the basic technique.

BELOW LEFT Irish crochet
BELOW RIGHT Filet crochet

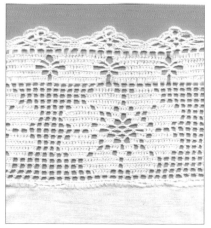

Question 5:
What equipment do I need?

The basic equipment for crochet is a hook and a ball of smooth yarn. A beginner needs a medium-size hook (F, G or H) with a light-colored soft and pliable yarn of worsted, or slightly thicker, weight.

Other useful tools include: a pair of scissors or yarn clippers, a tape measure, some sewing needles of different sizes, with large eyes and blunt points, a row counter and some glass-headed or quilters' pins, or a set of knitting clips to hold the edges together when sewing them. You may also like to keep a notebook and pen for any reminders you think you might need before you put your work away. A rigid ruler is useful for measuring gauge swatches. You might need some graph paper if you are making your own designs. Stitch markers and safety pins are useful, especially the coil-less ones if you can find them. For small pieces of crochet, it is handy to have a bag or purse of its own to keep it in. It's easy for crochet stitches to get pulled back if the yarn becomes snagged on anything in your work bag.

EXPERT TIP

❝ **Remove your hook and slip a safety pin through the last loop to prevent it from becoming unraveled when you put it away.** ❞

Question 6:
Are there different kinds of hook?

Hooks are sized by the diameter of the shaft, the straight part behind the point. They come in many sizes, from 14 (0.60mm) to 20.00mm. They are made from all kinds of material. The majority of midsize ones are made from aluminium, bamboo, or plastic but there are also hooks made from various types of wood, bone, ivory and even a milk protein, known as casein. The finer hooks are made from steel and are used to work the delicate pieces made from fine silk or cotton thread.

Until the advent of metrication, hook sizes were not standardized. There were different sizes for cotton and wool. Different manufacturers had their own gauges. It is not possible to interchange these older hooks or to expect to achieve the same gauge as that given in early patterns unless using the specific brand of hook stated in the pattern. But there are now standard sizes for hooks throughout the world, and a comparison table is given in the glossary at the end of the book.

Another difficulty with sizes is that some manufacturers make the point of the hook sharper while others make it more rounded, or the throat of the hook, the section within the curve of the point, will be broader in one brand than another. This can make quite a difference to the gauge obtained, so it is always important to do a gauge swatch.

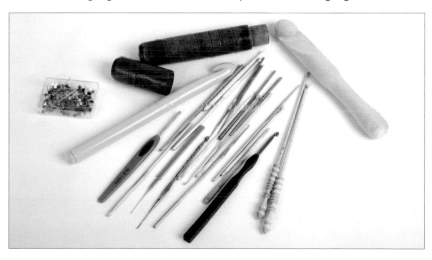

Question 7:
Why are some hooks a different shape?

The form of crochet known as Tunisian crochet, or Afghan crochet, is worked in a slightly different way than basic crochet. A number of stitches are collected on the hook before being worked off on the next row. This requires a longer hook and one that has a stopper at the end so that the stitches won't fall off.

Some of the newer hooks have a flexible cord, rather than being long and straight. These hooks are known as Tunisian or, sometimes, tricot hooks. They usually come in only medium to large sizes, but it is not impossible that some finer Tunisian hooks exist as there are examples of purses worked in this form of crochet using fine threads.

There are also double-ended hooks with a different size at each end. These are just a means of cutting down on the number of hooks you need, which is especially useful when traveling. But double-ended hooks with the same size at each end are a different matter—these are for working a form of Tunisian crochet in two colors.

Question 8:
Which is the best type of hook?

The best type of hook is the one that suits you best and feels most comfortable to work with, but there are certain decisions to be made before choosing one. Try to suit the hook to the type of yarn. A loosely spun yarn will be easier to work with if you use a more rounded hook, as this will not split the yarn. A hook with a sharper point will be useful for working with tightly spun or mercerized yarns because it will separate the strands of the stitches more easily and pass smoothly through the loops.

Another consideration is the material that the hook is made from. If you are using a very slippery yarn, such as silk or rayon, you may find it easier to work with a wooden hook that will not slide out of the loops. For other yarns, a bamboo hook with a smooth surface will slide easily in and out of the stitches. It also feels warmer to the touch than aluminium. Some people think this is easier to work with for those who have painful joints in their hands.

Hooks come in different lengths, and one brand may suit the size of your hand better than another. Not all hooks have thumb rests, although separate grips can be purchased that you slide over the handle. Whichever type of hooks you choose, look after them well, keep them clean by wiping occasionally with a damp cloth, and store them so that their points are protected. If they have rough edges, they will snag the yarn. It won't be as easy to slide them in and out of the stitches.

Question 9:
How can I tell the size of a hook if it is not marked?

While the sizes of hooks have been standardized, many of them will be labeled with only one of the designated sizes, metric, US or old UK. In most cases, the hook will have its size imprinted on the shank or the thumb grip, but this can wear off, especially from the plastic ones. To check the size, you will need to use a measuring gauge similar to the one used for knitting needles.

The most accurate ones are those with a tapered hole that you can slide the hook along, but a simple knitting needle gauge will do. Insert the hook into the hole that looks most likely to fit until it comes to rest just beyond the point, on the shank. Check the holes on either side of this too. The hook should not go right through the hole but should come to rest just inside it. Some of the older gauges, especially the bell gauge, have slots around the edge as well as holes, that are specifically for measuring crochet hooks, but the sizes given are those of the pre-metrication days. You will need to use a conversion table to find the modern-day equivalent. A table of hook sizes can be found at the back of this book.

LEFT Needle gauge.

Question 10:
How do I know which size hook to use?

If you are following a printed pattern, the instructions will tell you which size hook you should be using to obtain the same gauge as the designer. As was made clear in the previous question, hooks can vary from brand to brand, so always do a gauge swatch first.

If you are practicing, then you might find it best to start with a medium size – F, G or H – and a soft wool of worsted weight. Wool is more elastic than cotton and glides more easily over the hook than most synthetic fibers, so it is easier to work with.

If you are working a piece of crochet of your own design from a manufactured yarn, check the ball band for the suggested hook size. If it doesn't give crochet hook sizes, then use the equivalent size given for knitting needles to begin with. Where you are using a homespun yarn, or one that has no ball band, then you will need to work a few practice swatches until you find one that gives you the feel that you like best.

Alternatively, you can try passing two strands of your yarn through one of the holes in a measuring gauge. The one that they sit in most comfortably will be a guide to the size of hook to use.

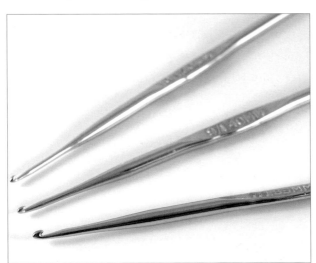

LEFT Hooks are available in a wide range of sizes.

Question 11:
What is yarn?

Yarn for crochet is the same as yarn for knitting. It is usually sold by weight in the form of hanks, skeins or balls, or sometimes on cardboard disks or tubes, especially in the case of silk and cotton. It can take many forms, from natural to synthetic, and is usually made by spinning one or more strands of fiber together (known as plying) to make various thicknesses of yarn.

Don't make the mistake of thinking that the number of plies of yarn will always equate to a particular thickness. A two-ply Shetland yarn is as thick as a sport or fingering weight wool, whereas a two-ply synthetic can be almost as fine as a one-ply cobweb yarn.

As well as yarns of one type of fiber, different fibers can be plied together to create mixed-fiber yarns. These are often a mix of wool and synthetic. Some of the new synthetics are very difficult to tell from natural fibers and can be just as pleasing to work with while usually being less expensive. However, although they can be machine washed and don't shrink, they do seem to attract dirt more readily and quickly lose their shape.

String, wire, plastic, leather, paper – all kinds of materials, although not strictly "yarn," are often used for crochet. Wire jewelry is becoming more familiar. Large pieces of artwork known as installations can be made from almost anything that can be formed into a continuous thread.

RIGHT Yarn is typically made from wool, but the term applies to many materials.

Question 12:
Which is the best type of yarn for crochet?

Wool and other plant and animal fibers are ideal to use for crochet. They are soft and flexible, making it easier to insert the hook into each of the stitches. These fibers will also give the fabric flexibility and the drape necessary for wearable items.

Like wool, alpaca yarns are also successfully used in crochet. Alpaca is a soft and warm yarn, but surprisingly it is not as elastic as wool. Also remember that there is not just one all-purpose wool. The wool of different breeds of sheep has varying properties; some are silky, some hairy, some soft and some coarse.

The yarn you choose should be determined by the function of the piece you are creating. Although natural fibers are pleasant to work with and to wear, they will not always put up with a lot of washing. If you are making items for babies and children, it might be better to choose a synthetic yarn or a cotton.

It is a good policy to choose a yarn that is fairly smooth, as this will show up the texture of the stitches to best advantage. Knobs and bumps can disguise the individual stitch, and the texture of crochet is one of

its features. Nubbly yarns are also difficult to work with as they will not pull through the stitches successfully. However, they can produce quite a pleasing overall fabric and it is worth experimenting, especially with a larger hook than you would normally use for such a yarn. Mohair and angora can also prove disappointing, as the longer hairs that are their characteristic will become lost as they are worked over by each successive stitch. However, this can be overcome to some extent if you, again, use a much larger hook than usual or work a very open and lacy pattern.

Question 13:
How much yarn will I need for a woman's sweater?

This is much the same as the "how long is a piece of string?" question — it depends to a large extent on the type of stitch that you are using. A sweater in an open lacy stitch will require much less yarn than one worked throughout in single crochet.

The instructions in a printed pattern are a good general guide, but it is always best to buy a ball or two more than that stated, especially as you can make a hat out of 3.5 ounces (100 g.) of spare yarn!

If you are working a design of your own, check the ball band for the length of yarn per ball, measure off a few yards of yarn and then work a piece of crochet in your chosen pattern. Measure this piece and work out approximately how many pieces of the same size will fit into your design. Then calculate the number of yards of yarn you will need to complete it and how many balls this will mean. This will be only a rough guide, so buy a couple of extra balls. When trying to decide if you will have enough yarn left to finish a sweater, it will take approximately one-third for the back, one-third for the front and one-third for both sleeves. Remember to reserve a bit for the collar and/or front bands.

RIGHT A crocheted woman's sweater in an open lacy stitch.

LEFT Choose your yarn according to the type of garment you are making, its purpose, and the look you want to achieve.

Question 14:
Which yarn should I use for household items?

This is where the fun starts. Depending on the item, any kind of fiber can be used. Plastic can make useful shopping bags, as can hemp, string or twine, which can also be used to make a sturdy rug. String is also ideal for making baskets and containers. Strips of leather, while quite expensive, make stylish-looking floor cushions. Cashmere and alpaca, being light and warm, make cozy afghans, and linen, which drapes well, can be used to make chic curtains. All kinds of fibers are suitable for cushion covers, which are subject to less washing. One of the reasons that crochet gained in popularity in the Victorian and Edwardian eras was the easy availability of cotton. Although there are artificial substitutes, it can't really be surpassed for making delicate edgings on sheets and pillowcases or for such heirloom pieces as tablecloths and bedspreads.

Crochet cotton is produced in a range of thicknesses suitable for many purposes, from 3 to 100, with the higher number denoting the finer thread. It also comes in a variety of colors, including variegated and space dyed, although the finest threads are usually available in only white or ecru.

Question 15:
How do I crochet with wire?

The wire typically used for crochet is known as scientific wire, but you can use any you find in the house or garage. Scientific wire comes in a variety of weights and colors and is sold by the length or on spools, like sewing cotton. Like crochet cotton, the higher the number, the thinner the wire, but 28 or 30 is probably the most suitable as it is the most flexible but not so fine it will snap. It is often used to make jewelry and is worked with a strong metal hook.

It is not easy to unravel wire, so learn to live with your mistakes; they probably won't show anyway. It will break if you pull on it too hard. So try to make each stitch just the right size, don't keep pulling to tighten the stitches. You will need to maneuver the wire over the hook. It's not flexible enough to allow the hook to catch it.

Crochet with wire can be hard on the fingers, so it's best to do it in short bursts or wear a finger guard. Some people find a long thimble useful or adhesive bandage!

Question 16:
Can I convert a knitting pattern to crochet?

It is possible to do this, although the item will probably have a different drape. You will need graph paper and several gauge swatches.

Check the gauge of the knitting pattern. Using the same size hook as the size of knitting needles required, make a swatch in one of the basic stitches and try to get the same number of stitches as in the gauge of the knitting pattern. Keep changing hook, yarn and stitch until you make a gauge as close as possible to the original number of stitches. Don't worry about rows for the moment, as crochet stitches are invariably taller.

Draw the design on graph paper, using a square for each stitch. From your gauge swatch, work out how many rows you will need to achieve the length. Adjust any multiples of increasing and decreasing to fit the shape. As crochet uses more yarn, do remember to buy extra.

2
HOW TO START

Once you are comfortable with your tools, the first step is to
make the foundation chain — how to judge its length and begin
work on it is described over the following pages.

Question 17:
How do I hold the hook?

These instructions are written as though you are right-handed. If you are left-handed, hold the hook and the yarn in just the same way, but read right for left and vice versa.

There are two ways of holding the hook. In both cases, one hand holds the hook and the other guides and

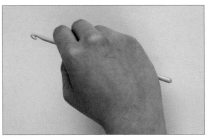

tensions the yarn. The first way is to grip it as if it were a pen, with the thumb and forefinger about 1 inch (2.5 cm) down the shank from the hook end and with the rest of the shank lying along the top of the hand to the right of the thumb joint.

The second is to hold it like a knife, with the thumb and forefinger gripping the shank somewhere near the center, or on the flat part, and with the rest of the shank in the palm of the hand.

These are the most familiar ways of holding the hook, but you may find another that you feel more comfortable with. You may even change your hold depending on which stitch you are working. Whichever way feels most comfortable and gives you the most even tension is the best way to hold it.

LEFT Two ways of holding the hook.

Question 18:
How do I hold the yarn?

There is also more than one way of holding the yarn. You are aiming for a slight tension, enough to keep it

within the throat of the hook but not so tight that it is difficult to pull from the ball nor so loose that it makes large, uneven stitches. Hold the yarn in the opposite hand to the hook and have the ball on that side of your body. Loop the yarn once around your little finger, under your two middle fingers and over your forefinger. As you work, take the yarn from the front of your forefinger and let it flow freely across your palm from the little finger and back to the ball. Use your middle finger and thumb to hold the stitches you have made, moving along the stitches closer to the hook as you work.

An alternative way of holding the yarn is around the little finger, under the fourth finger and over the middle finger, holding the work with your thumb and forefinger and taking yarn from the front of the middle finger.

Keep moving your thumb and finger along the stitches you have made, toward the hook, to make it easier to keep the live stitch open. If you find the yarn is not running as freely as you would like, omit the wrap around the little finger and keep the ball end in your palm.

Question 19:
How do I make the first stitch?

Before beginning a piece of crochet, you first need to make a loop of yarn, called a slipknot, on your hook. A simple way to do this is to make a small circle of yarn, with the end from the ball passing over the top and behind the circle. With the hook, or with your fingers if you find it easier, pull the end joined to the ball from back to front, through the circle. Pull on both ends of the

yarn to draw the knot up tight but still leave it movable so that you can work the next stitch into it.

Where you want the slipknot to close up tightly, as at the beginning of a circular piece of crochet, for example, take the end that is not joined to the ball through the loop. Pulling on this after you have finished the work will make the hole much smaller.

Once you have seen how the slipknot works, it is a simple matter to make one by wrapping the yarn around the hook and then drawing a loop through. This movement forms the basis of all crochet stitches.

LEFT Making a slipknot.

Question 20:
How do I start a piece of crochet?

Starting a piece of crochet is the equivalent to casting on when you are knitting. Most pieces start with a series of chain stitches, which is known as a foundation chain, or a base chain that is worked onto the slipknot.

To work the foundation chain, begin by holding the tail end of the yarn firmly between your thumb and finger and then wrap the yarn, from the ball end, back to front over the hook, by passing the hook in front of the yarn and guiding the yarn into the throat.

Holding the yarn in the throat of the hook, draw the hook back through the slipknot, bringing a loop of yarn with it. This makes one chain. The rest of the foundation chain is made by repeating these movements, wrapping the yarn and drawing it back each time, until you have the required number of

BELOW Inserting the hook in the slipknot.

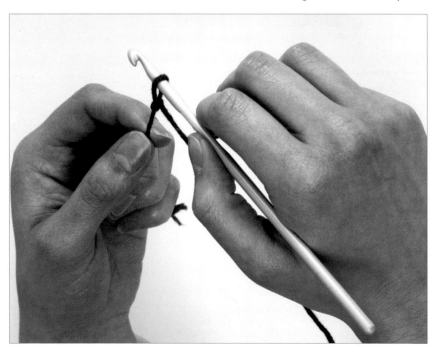

chain stitches to begin your crochet.

A handy tip, when making your foundation chain, is to move your finger and thumb along the chains and nearer to the hook as you work in order to keep an even tension as you go.

Neither the slipknot, nor the loop that is on the hook, are actually counted as a stitch. If the instructions you are following state that you should "begin with 24 chains," this means that after you have placed the slipknot on the hook, you work one chain stitch after another until you have 24 of them in total.

It is usually easiest to count the stitches as you go. If you happen to lose count, simply start at the slipknot. While making sure that the chain is not twisted, count each of the "V" shapes that appear on the chain, all the way back to the hook.

An alternative method to begin a piece of crochet is one that is sometimes used when you are working in rounds. In this method, the yarn is simply wrapped a number of times around your finger or a pencil and then the first crochet stitch is made into the center of this ring.

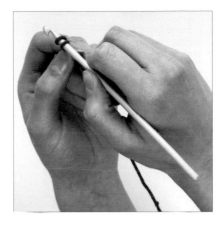

TOP Yarn on the hook ready to draw through the slipknot.

BOTTOM The first few chain stiches are made.

Question 21:
What if I make the foundation chain too short?

The number of chain stitches you need to make in your foundation row is always more than the number of stitches you have in your first row. This is because the first two or three stitches actually take the place of your first stitch, that is, the one at the outside edge of the piece. You then skip the next chain before working into the following one, or as instructed in the pattern.

To begin a piece that does not give explicit instructions for the number of chain stitches in the foundation row, count the stitches, including spaces if there are any, in the first row then add on the appropriate number of stitches for the turning chain.

If you have miscalculated and run out of chain stitches before completing the first row, you will have to add on a few extra ones. If you have left a long tail when making the slipknot, you may be able to use this. Otherwise, you will need to join in a new piece of yarn.

To do this, insert the hook into the slipknot and then continue making chain stitches until you have the correct number. Cut off the yarn and fasten it off. These new chains will face in the opposite direction but won't be noticeable in the finished piece, especially if you are adding an edging to the foundation row. In this case, you can work over the extra tail ends as you work, saving the job of darning them in later.

Alternatively, fasten off the yarn, leaving a long tail, before starting your first row. Then rejoin yarn to slipknot end and work back along the row, going under each of the ridges and the strand behind them. It is then simple to add on a few more chain stitches before completing the row.

Question 22:
What if I make the foundation chain too long?

If you find you have worked too many chains before working the first row, it is a simple matter to slip the hook out of the last loop and pull back on the yarn to undo the extra ones. If you complete your first row and have several chains left over at the end, you can undo them from the slipknot. Using a needle or a finer hook, tease out the knot and the end of yarn from each successive surplus stitch. Pull the tail end of yarn to draw it close to the next

BELOW Starting from the "wrong" end of the foundation chain.

true stitch. Many older patterns didn't state the number of chains to be worked in a foundation row but merely gave instructions for a chain of a certain length. Workers would get around this by making it too long and removing the extra chains on completing the work. There are some old pieces in existence where the surplus chain is still intact!

You could also start your first row at the other end of the chain. Break off the yarn, and fasten a safety pin to the last stitch. If you have too many left, simply remove the safety pin and undo them.

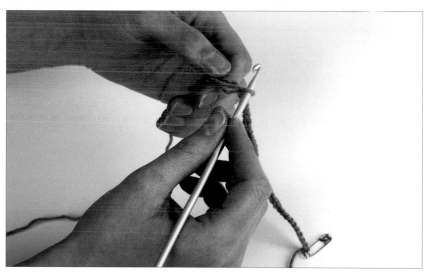

Question 23:
Are there any other ways to start a piece of crochet?

A standard foundation chain is not the only method of beginning your piece of crochet. There are also alternative foundation chains. The first one more resembles a braid and is worked over two stitches. It is known as double foundation chain.

Begin with two foundation chains. Insert the hook into the first one, wrap the yarn over the hook and draw it through, wrap the yarn over the hook again and draw it through both loops.

Turn the work counterclockwise. You will see two strands of yarn side by side, pointing to the left and looking like a small knot. Next, insert the hook downward under both of these strands, wrap the yarn over the hook and draw it through, then wrap the yarn over again and draw it through both loops.

Turn the work counterclockwise again and repeat the procedure as before, doing so until your chain is long enough to work with.

You will find that, if you turn

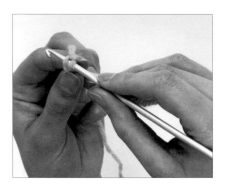

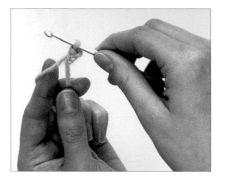

RIGHT Three stages in making a double foundation chain.

the work in opposite directions each time, the foundation chain you end up with will have a slightly different appearance on each side. Nevertheless, either side of the chain can be used as the right side when you begin working your crochet pattern.

An alternative method, which can be very useful because it forms your first row at the same time, is as described below. These alternative foundation chains can be used in place of the standard one whenever you wish. They make it easier to work into the first row and are also less likely to curl. They will be slightly heavier but more elastic than the simple foundation chain. They are useful for edges that need a bit of stretch, such as cuffs and hat brims.

1 To begin, make two chains and then insert the hook into the first one that you made, yarn over hook. Draw it through, yarn over hook again, and then draw it through the two loops that you just made.

2 Insert the crochet hook into the second stitch and repeat the procedure for the first stitch. You can also work this chain using any of the other basic stitches instead of single crochet.

Question 24:
How do I work into the foundation chain?

Assuming that your first row is one of single crochet, the method of working into a standard foundation chain is to insert the hook under two strands of the second chain from the hook and work one single crochet (see page 46 for instructions on how to work this stitch).

Insert the hook into the next chain along and work another single crochet. Repeat this action, working one single crochet into each chain, always inserting the hook under two strands each time.

If you find this awkward to work, try making your foundation chain a little looser or insert the hook under only one strand of the chain each time. You could also try inserting

the hook under the little ridge that forms on the back of the chains. Do be consistent. Don't go under one strand one time and under two on another stitch, or under the front one and then under a back one. Any of these methods will give you a firm, straight edge, which is what you are aiming for.

If you are working from a pattern, you may be instructed to miss one or more chains along the row to form a series of arches or spaces. Where this is the case, work the straightforward foundation chain rather than one of the alternative ones.

BELOW Working a single crochet into the foundation chain.

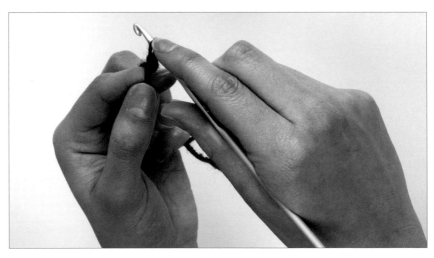

Question 25:
Do I need to make a gauge swatch?

Whether you are following a pattern or designing one of your own, you should always make a gauge swatch so that you know exactly how many stitches and rows are contained in 1 inch (2.5 cm), or how many stitches and rows it takes to make a particular segment of the pattern. Even being half a stitch off can make a huge difference to your finished measurement and be totally unsuitable for the wearer. The number of stitches could also affect the quantity of yarn required, as you will need more if it takes you more stitches and rows to achieve the given measurements.

To make your gauge swatch, use the hook size and stitch quoted in the pattern and make a piece at least 6 inches (15 cm) square. When you have made your swatch, block and press it according to the instructions on the ball band, leave it to rest, then lay it on a flat surface and measure across 4 inches (10 cm), (or the amount suggested in the pattern) with a rigid ruler. Mark this section with pins and count the number of stitches between them. Do the same for the rows and count them too. Include partial stitches and rows too.

There are many reasons why you may not be able to obtain the correct gauge. You could be sitting in an uncomfortable position. You may be using the correct yarn but in a different color than that of the pattern. Different dyes can affect the thickness of a yarn. The yarn may be difficult to pull from the ball, or you may simply have rougher hands than normal. If you are working a new stitch, you will probably work tighter than when you become more used to it. As you become accustomed to the pattern, you speed up, and this often results in looser stitches. If you try to maintain an even speed throughout the piece, your gauge should remain the same.

If you can't match the gauge exactly, try using a different brand of hook. The thickness of the neck and the shape of the point can vary from one brand to another. This will all affect the end result. You could also try holding the yarn in a different way, wrapping it around the ring finger as well as the little finger if your stitches are too loose or not wrapping it around your finger at all if they are too tight.

Question 26:
How do I count the stitches?

With almost all crochet stitches you will try, you'll find that, when you have completed a series of them, you will be able to see a row of "V"s lying along the top of the work. Tilt it slightly toward you to be able to see them better.

Each of these "V"s is one stitch. If you are working clusters of stitches – in other words, in stitches that are gathered together at the top – count each cluster as one stitch. If you are working shells or similar patterns where stitches are grouped together at the base, then count the number of shells and half shells. The printed pattern will usually indicate how many shells or blocks of a pattern are required to achieve a specific measurement.

At the end of a row, there will be a stitch that does not look like its neighbors. This is the turning chain, which is also counted as a stitch, unless the pattern says otherwise. The loop that is on your hook is not counted as a stitch.

Get into the habit of counting the stitches as you make them until you become familiar with how the last one should look.

BELOW Each "V" shape on your finished work represents one stitch.

Question 27:
How do I count the rows?

If you have been working one of the basic stitches, turning the work at the end of each row, the rows will appear as pairs. One row will seem to be slightly raised and one depressed. Count these rows in their pairs and then add on the odd one if it occurs.

Where you are working a piece of crochet that is a lacy or shell pattern, the gauge may not be given in terms of x rows = 4 inches, but as 1 pattern = x inches. To be most accurate with your measurements, work the pattern stitch at least twice – three times would be better – and then measure over the central portion to check that your pattern block is the same size as that given in the instructions.

Measure from the base of one row to the base of another, which may not always be a square when you are working a pattern that produces waves. Make sure that as you are counting, you don't miss any rows that consist entirely of chain loops, especially where other rows are worked over them.

You can always work rows more or less in the straight part of a piece in order to obtain the required length. The difficulty comes when you are instructed to work shaping a certain number of times, as in an armhole and sleeve cap. You can remedy this fairly simply on a raglan sleeve, but the sleeve cap of a set-in sleeve is shaped differently to the armhole on the body. On the body, you will be instructed to work to a certain length, which the designer assumes will take a particular number of rows. This number is matched to the number of rows in the sleeve cap. If you alter one, you will need to calculate how to shape the other.

EXPERT TIP

66 **If you are finding it difficult to achieve the exact number of stitches and rows as that quoted in the pattern, it is more important for your finished measurements to get the number of stitches right.** 99

Question 28:
How do I tell which is the right side?

When you have finished your foundation chain, there will be a tail of yarn at the beginning. The foundation row is not normally counted as the first row so, when you turn your work to begin the first row, this tail will be at the left-hand end. Every time you have the tail end at the left, you have the right side of the work facing you. For left-handers, the reverse will apply. The right side will be the one where the tail end is at the right-hand end.

However, the majority of crochet stitches are reversible, so it is up to you to decide which is the right or wrong side. Remember that there can be a slight difference in the nap on one side or the other. If you are making up a garment of several pieces, examine them carefully to check that you have worked the shapings in the correct place to achieve a left and right front.

When you are working in the round, you will almost always have the right side facing you. If you have to turn the work after each round, there may be a distinct right and wrong side. If there is no easy way to distinguish this, tie a piece of colored yarn to one of the stitches on the wrong side.

BELOW Tail end of yarn at left, showing the right side of the chain.

Question 29:
How do I make a straight piece of fabric?

After you have finished making your foundation chain and worked the first row, turn the work around so that what was the wrong side is now facing you.

Make a number of chains so that the hook is at the same height as the stitches that will follow it. Each of the basic stitches is a different height. The hook needs to be ready at the same height as the stitch that will come next in order to keep a horizontal line (unless you are working a pattern that instructs differently). The correct number of chains for each of the most common stitches is given in the table below.

Make your first stitch into what would be the second chain along after making the turning chains. Remember that the turning chain counts as one stitch, so don't forget to work into it at the end of the row.

There are some occasions when the pattern instructions will dictate a specific number of turning chains, but otherwise follow the numbers in the table. There are also some patterns that instruct you not to count the turning chain as a stitch. In this case, you will work the turning chains and then work the first stitch into the stitch that they stand on. This method does not give such a straight edge as the first one.

When turning your work, always turn it in the same direction so it will be easy to see which is the top stitch of the turning chain for you to work into at the end of the row.

Name of stitch	No. of turning chain
Slip stitch	None
Single crochet	1
Half double crochet	2
Double crochet	3
Triple	4
Double triple	5

3
BASIC STITCHES

The four basic stitches in crochet are chain stitch, slip stitch, single crochet and double crochet. Mastering these will give you the skills to tackle almost any crochet pattern.

Question 30:
What are the basic stitches?

There are only four basic stitches in crochet. These are chain stitch, slip stitch, single crochet and double crochet. Other stitches are only variations on these.

These few basic stitches combine to make an infinite number of patterns, some simple and some that look intricate, but are worked in the same way. Once you have mastered the basic skills, you will be able to create a multitude of patterns.

The chain stitch is the foundation on which most crochet stitches are based and is made up of only one movement. When you have built up a rhythm for working chain stitches, you will find almost all of the other stitches will come naturally. Practice lengths of chains until you are making them in one smooth movement and can get all of the stitches the same size. All crochet stitches have some height, with chain stitches being the shallowest, followed by slip stitch, single crochet then double crochet. There are various kinds of longer stitches known as triples.

BELOW One row of single alternated with one row of double crochet. The lower half is worked between the stitches; the upper half is worked as normal.

Question 31:
How do I make a chain stitch?

To begin a row of chain stitches, you first need to make a slipknot as described in Chapter 2. Once you have this slipknot in place, you can make your first chain from it.

Wrap the yarn from the back of the hook to the front so that it sits in the throat of the hook, then pull it through the slipknot. This makes one chain. Continue working in this way, wrapping the yarn from back to front each time and drawing the hook back through the loop until you feel comfortable with working these stitches and they are all the same size. Don't pull them too tightly or it will be difficult to work

into them for your first row. As you become more familiar with the way of working, you will be able to catch the yarn with the hook rather than wrapping it around. This will be a much faster way of working.

Chain stitches make up the foundation row that is the basis of most straight pieces of crochet and equivalent to the cast-on row in knitting. They are also used alone to form mesh patterns or with other stitches for a variety of decorative fabrics.

BELOW A loop of yarn ready to draw through to make one chain stitch.

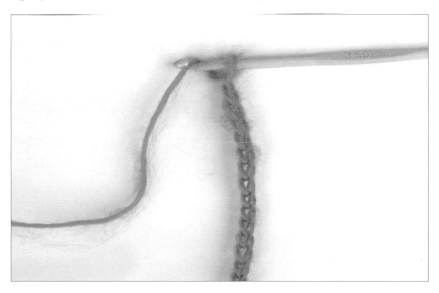

Question 32:
How do I work the first row?

The first row of crochet is often the most difficult to work. It can sometimes help to use a larger-size hook for the foundation row than you are going to use for the body of the work.

When you have made your row of chains, tip them toward you slightly and you will see that each stitch is made up of three strands: what looks like a row of "V"s at the front and a ridge at the back. The most usual way of working into the foundation chain is to insert the hook from front to back under two strands of the chain, the top leg of the "V" and the ridge from the back. This leaves one strand from the bottom leg of the "V" for the "cast-on" edge. Occasionally, a pattern instruction will require you to insert the hook under one strand only; this usually means the top strand of the "V" but will sometimes mean the ridge from the back.

Always read the instructions through carefully. If there are no specific instructions, then always insert the hook under the top two strands. After you have made the first stitch into the appropriate chain, insert the hook into every chain along the row and work in your chosen stitch to the end.

If you are working an open or lacy pattern, the instructions may require you to miss a number of chains between each stitch. Count these by counting the number of "V"s along the foundation chain.

BELOW Working single crochet into the foundation chain.

Question 33:
How do I work a slip stitch?

Slip stitch is the shortest of the basic stitches. It can be used to form a firm edge to a piece of crochet, to join a round, to move across the fabric to a new starting point, or as a decorative stitch on top of an existing piece of crochet. It is very rarely used on its own to form a whole crochet fabric.

To work slip stitch, insert the hook from the front to the back into the second chain from the hook, wrap the yarn over the hook from back to front, as for a chain stitch, and draw the yarn through the chain and the existing loop on the hook in one movement. This is one slip stitch.

Insert the hook into the next chain and repeat the process so that you end up with one loop on the hook each time and a row of short but firm stitches along the top of the foundation chain. The technique may seem difficult at first. If you haven't made your foundation chain too tight, it will be easy to see where to insert the hook in each chain.

BELOW A series of slip stitches worked into the foundation chain.

Question 34:
How do I work single crochet?

Single crochet is the simplest and shortest of the true fabric stitches. It is sometimes known as a short stitch. It is a firm stitch and makes a fabric that looks the same on both sides. It is worked in two stages.

Make a simple foundation chain and insert the hook into the second chain as before. Wrap the yarn over and draw it through the chain. You will now have two loops on your hook. Wrap the yarn over the hook again and draw it through both of these loops at once. You have now made one single crochet. Insert the hook into the next chain, yarn over hook, draw it through, yarn over

hook again and draw it through both loops. Repeat these movements to the end of the row or until you are comfortable working this stitch.

To make the second row, turn the work so the left-hand end is now at the right. Begin the next row. Make one chain, then insert the hook into the second stitch, under the two strands along the top of the row, bring the yarn over the hook from front to back, draw it through and complete the stitch as for the first row. Work a number of rows, turning the work each time.

BELOW Rows of single crochet.

Question 35:
Which is the second stitch?

After you have worked a complete row of crochet, you will notice that there is one loop left on the hook. This loop will form the top of your next stitch, but bear in mind that it is not counted as a stitch until it is completed.

Turn the work around so that what was the reverse side of the piece is now facing you. What was the last stitch of the row has now become the base of the first stitch of the next row. Make a number of chains to stand for your first stitch.

These set of chains are called a turning chain. Don't work into the stitch that these chains are standing on. Work into the next stitch along from the hook, in other words, the second stitch. This method of working will give a straight edge to your crochet.

If you are working in single crochet, you will find that it is sometimes recommended that you work into the first stitch as well as making a turning chain. The one turning chain that you make for this stitch gives very little height or width and will not have much effect on the evenness of the edges. However, any of the longer stitches are best worked into the second stitch after working the appropriate number of turning chains.

Some patterns will instruct you to work into the stitch that the turning chain stands on. You will notice, if you do this, that the edges of the work are not as straight as those where the turning chain is counted as the first stitch. If the work is to be seamed or trimmed with an edging, this won't matter as the irregularities can be hidden in the seam or edging. If the work is not to be joined or edged, use the method of working outlined above. Whichever method you choose, be consistent or it will be difficult to keep count of the stitches.

EXPERT TIP

66 **Count your stitches for a few rows and constantly look at your work. You will familiarize yourself with the lay of the stitches and the way each one appears.** 99

Question 36:
Which is the last stitch?

The last stitch of the row is the loop that was at the top of the turning chain you made at the beginning. It will look slightly different than the other stitches.

If you find that you are gradually losing stitches as you work subsequent rows, then you are probably missing this stitch. As you work, count the stitches that you make. If you have one less than required, look at the edge of the work and see if you can find a chain loop that has not been worked into. This will be your last stitch.

Insert the hook under the two loops that lie more or less horizontally along the top of the turning chain. If you always turn your work in the same direction at the end of each row, this last stitch will always appear the same and you will eventually recognize where to insert the hook to make the last stitch.

Question 37:
How do I make double crochet?

The double crochet stitch is probably the most widely used stitch in crochet – it forms the basis of many of the pattern stitches as well as being the primary stitch in filet crochet. It is worked in three stages. Like single crochet, if worked on every row, the fabric will appear the same on both sides. It is a little more open than single crochet and has a softer drape. It is the stitch that makes the majority of crochet patterns and is worked as follows.

ABOVE Rows of double crochet.

HOW IT'S DONE

1 Wrap the yarn around the hook and insert the hook into the 4th chain from the hook.

2 Wrap the yarn around again and draw it through this chain; you will now have 3 loops on the hook.

3 Wrap the yarn around again and draw it through the first 2 loops on the hook.

4 Wrap the yarn around again and draw it through the remaining 2 loops on the hook.

One loop is left on the hook. You have made a double crochet.

Repeat these four stages to the end of the row.

When you reach the end of the row, turn the work, make 3 chains to stand as the first double crochet and then work 1 double crochet into the next chain.

Continue to work one double crochet into every chain to the end of the row, not forgetting to work into the top chain at the end of the row (in other words, your last stitch).

RIGHT From the top: Initial yarn wrapover; hook inserted into stitch and yarn being wrapped over a second time; yarn in throat of hook ready to be drawn through first two loops; two loops on hook and yarn ready to be wrapped over again; and completed stitch.

Question 38:
How do I make a half double crochet?

A half double crochet is longer than a single crochet and shorter than a double crochet. It is worked in three stages. It is another firm fabric stitch. By being taller than a single crochet stitch but shorter than the double, it is often used to decrease or increase an arch shape gradually in a pattern. It is simple to make, whether or not you are already comfortable with the single and double crochet stitches. Practice, however, will help you to keep them straight. This is best done using a medium-sized crochet hook and solid plain or worsted weight yarn.

HOW IT'S DONE

1 Wrap the yarn around the hook and insert it into the third chain along.

2 Wrap the yarn around the hook again and then draw it through the foundation chain stitch, giving you 3 loops.

3 Wrap the yarn around the crochet hook again and draw it through all 3 loops.

One loop should be left on the hook. You have made a half double crochet.

You may find it easier to draw the hook through all 3 loops if you twist the hook toward you and downward slightly.

Wrap the yarn around the hook and insert it into the next chain. Complete the stitch as you did for the first half double.

Repeat these movements all along the foundation chain, working once into every stitch for a row of half double crochet.

RIGHT Rows of half double crochet.

Question 39:
How do I make a triple crochet?

Triple crochet, which is also sometimes known as treble crochet, is the first of the longer stitches. It is not often used on its own to form a complete fabric but is frequently worked as part of a pattern, especially when making shells. It makes looser patterns than the stitches described previously and is useful when you want to make something soft and fluid. The triple crochet is worked as follows.

RIGHT Consecutive rows of triples.

HOW IT'S DONE

1 After making a foundation chain, begin the triple crochet stitch by wrapping the yarn twice around the hook.

2 Insert the hook into the fifth chain from the hook.

3 Wrap the yarn around the hook and draw it through this chain. This will give you 4 loops on the hook.

4 Wrap the yarn around the hook again and draw it through 2 loops, leaving 3 loops on the hook.

5 Wrap the yarn around again and draw it through 2 loops, leaving 2 loops on the hook.

6 Wrap the yarn around the hook again and draw it through the last 2 loops.

7 This makes one triple.

8 Repeat these movements all along the foundation chain, wrapping the yarn twice around the hook before each stitch and working into every stitch along the row.

9 Make 4 chains to turn, ready for the next row of triples.

Question 40:
How do I make a double triple?

Like the triple crochet, double triples are not often used on their own but form part of a pattern. On their own, they make a loose fabric that could be used for attractive scarves and stoles. They are usually used in combination with other stitches for lacy patterns.

They are made in the same way as triples, but wrap the yarn three times around the hook. If you are starting from a foundation chain, insert the hook into the sixth chain. The first five chains bring your hook up to the required height. Draw the yarn through the sixth chain, making

five loops on the hook. Wrap the yarn over again and draw the yarn through two loops. Repeat this last procedure, leaving one less loop on the hook each time, until all the loops are worked off.

You can continue, ad infinitum, making longer and longer triples by wrapping the yarn more and more times around the hook before working the loops off in twos. These very long stitches are not stable when used alone and can easily get caught and snagged. However, they do make the work grow quickly and are perhaps more useful when working with thick yarns and big hooks.

BELOW Working a double triple.

Question 41:
What is an extended stitch?

Apart from slip stitch, any of the stitches described in the questions so far can be turned into extended stitches, also known as locked stitches. The method of working is the same for each of the stitches. The instructions which follow for extended double crochet will demonstrate the principle of working.

These extended stitches are useful where you don't want a loose open stitch but would like your fabric to have a little more drape than it does when worked in one of the basic stitches.

The technique works on any of the stitches made up of more than two stages, that is, anything longer than a single crochet. The stitch is begun in the normal way but then an extra move is made, drawing the hook through one loop of yarn only before completing the stitch as normal.

Extended stitches are an intermediate stage between the height of the normal stitch and the next tallest one. The heights of the stitches in ascending order are slip stitch, single crochet, half double crochet, double crochet, extended double crochet, half triple, triple,

extended triple (which could actually be extended twice), then triple triple, extended triple triple, and so on.

NB: These stitches will all be shorter if they are worked around the post.

HOW IT'S DONE

1 Wrap the yarn over the crochet hook and insert the hook into the relevant stitch.

2 Wrap the yarn over again and draw it through the stitch, giving 3 loops on the hook.

3 Wrap the yarn over the crochet hook again and draw it through one loop so that you still have 3 loops on the hook.

4 Wrap the yarn over the crochet hook again and then complete the stitch as for normal double crochet; that is, by drawing it through 2 loops at a time until only 1 is left on the hook.

5 For all of the other variations, draw the yarn through 1 loop the first time, leaving you with the same number of loops on the hook as there were when taking it through the first chain or stitch. Then complete the stitch as normal.

Question 42:
When would I use each of the stitches?

All of the main crochet stitches, when used on their own row by row, will produce a simple fabric that is the same on both sides. Even when they are used as part of a pattern, it will often be difficult to determine the right or wrong side of the work.

For this reason, these types of stitches are useful for making such items as scarves and throws, where the wrong side will sometimes be on show. Single crochet, half double and double crochet are all fairly firm stitches that are suitable for jackets. They can all be used alone or in combination with other stitches. The simplest patterns are formed by working one of the basic stitches followed by one or two chains in place of solid stitches. This will give a more open look to the fabric but will still work to the same gauge as using the basic stitch alone. The longer stitches are best used in combination with others to form a variety of patterns. Long stitches do have a tendency to drop, especially if you are working a heavy garment. Before you finish the piece, hang it up overnight to let the stitches settle into place.

Slip stitch is not a true pattern stitch, but it has a number of uses. It is used either to move the hook along the row ready to work the next stitch or as a form of binding off, as in shaping armholes or necklines. It is also used to form picots and in circular crochet, to move to the correct point for the next part of the pattern. Slip stitch can also be used to make cords and braids. How it is used to make cords is described on page 214.

EXPERT TIP

66 **Slip stitch, chain stitch and single crochet can also be used to join seams or to finish off a piece of crochet with a simple edging that will neaten necklines or armholes.** 99

Question 43:
What is a chain space?

Basic stitches can be made more decorative and open by working a chain stitch between them and missing a stitch before working the next one. If you don't miss a stitch you will increase the width of the piece, useful when making shawls or circular pieces. The chain stitch above a missed stitch will make a small hole, called the chain space. If you need to work into it on the next row, work directly into the space beneath the chain stitch rather than into the head of the stitch. You can work any number of chains and

miss the corresponding number of stitches, working that number into this gap on the next row. However many chains you make, the hole is referred to as a chain space although there is more than one chain in the group. Some patterns may attach a number, such as three-chain space.

Working chains between stitches in this way forms many easy-to-work patterns. The simplest is chain spaces and single crochet, which makes an open mesh fabric suitable for using all over to make string bags or simple decorative edging for cuffs, necklines and hems. It is a simple way to increase stitches to make triangular pieces suitable for shawls.

BELOW Shawl made using single crochet and five-chain pieces.

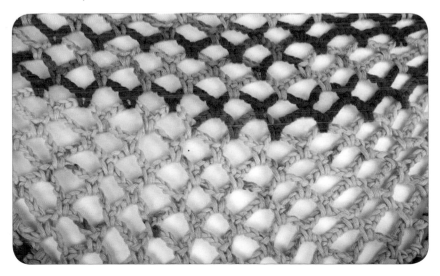

Question 44:
What is the post, or stem?

The post, also known as the stem, of a stitch is the vertical section of any of the stitches longer than a slip stitch. You will notice that the slip stitch has no vertical section and just forms a "V" directly on top of the previous chain or stitch.

All of the other stitches, which includes single crochet, have varying lengths of post. Single crochet is simply two threads side by side. All of the others appear to have a number of threads twisted together.

BELOW A post, or stem, in a piece of crochet.

There are times when a pattern will require you to work around the post rather than into the top of the stitch, and this technique is described in the next question. It makes the stitch stand out in relief, or retreat into the background, and is a way of giving more texture to a plain fabric.

Working into the post is also useful when you are working an edging along the side of a piece of crochet. It makes a neater edge to your finished piece of crochet if you work into the post of each row rather than into the space alongside the stitch.

Question 45:
How do I work around the post?

You can work around either the front or the back of the post. To work one double crochet around the front of a row of stitches, wrap the yarn around the hook, insert the hook from the front, through the gap between the two stitches, behind the stitch, and back through the next gap from back to front as if weaving the hook through the stitches.

Wrap the yarn over the hook and complete the stitch as for a normal double crochet. Repeat this action along the row, inserting the hook from the front to the back each time.

To work around the back of the post, follow the instructions above, but take the hook from the back, across the front of the post and into the gap between the stitches to the back of the work.

Working in blocks of five or six stitches around the front and five or six around the back will give a sort of basket weave effect to your fabric.

The stitch that is formed by working around the post, rather than into the top of it, is known as a relief stitch.

BELOW Working around the back of the post.

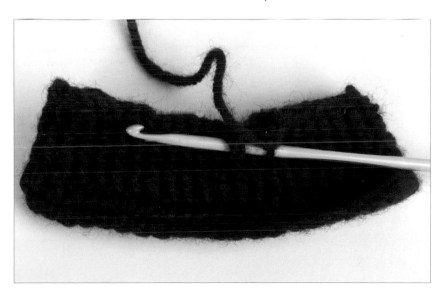

Question 46:
What does "work 2 stitches together" mean?

To "work 2 stitches together" means to turn two stitches into one, either to decrease or to form part of a pattern. The method of working is to begin the stitch in the normal way but not to complete it. In other words, omit the last movement.

For example, to work 2 single crochet together, insert the hook into the next stitch, yarn around hook and draw through, insert the hook into the following stitch, yarn around hook and draw through to make 3 loops on the hook, yarn around hook and draw through all three loops, closing them together. This can be abbreviated to either 2sctog or sc2tog.

Any of the stitches can be decreased in this way, and any number can be decreased together. Work them as usual until the last movement. Then work into the next stitch and draw the yarn through the remaining loops on the hook at the end of that stitch. They can be worked together at the beginning of the row or anywhere else along the row. When worked at the beginning and end of the row, they will leave a neat slope rather than a series of steps, which you would get by simply missing the first or last stitch. Working the stitches together in this way also keeps a uniform pattern and prevents the small hole that you would get if you missed a stitch.

BELOW Two stitches worked together.

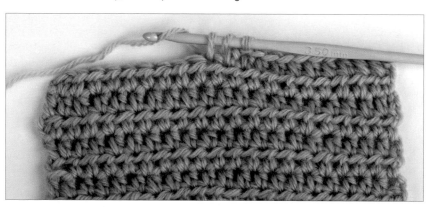

Question 47:
How do I work into the back loop only?

If you take your piece of crochet with the right side facing you and tilt it toward you, you will see what looks like a line of horizontal "v"s or small chain links along the top. Each crochet stitch is normally worked under both strands of these "v"s to form the basic fabric stitches.

However, the appearance of the pattern can be changed by working under the rear part of the "v" only – the one farthest away from you, known as the back loop. This will result in a series of ridges between each row. This way of working can be applied to every row or to only those rows on one side of the work. The different methods will result in a different appearance.

You can also work into the front loops only. Either way of working will give a slightly softer, more flexible fabric than if you worked under the two loops.

Another alternative is to work under the back loop of the first stitch and the front loop of the second. Each way of working will give a different appearance to a basic stitch.

Question 48:
What is a "linked" stitch?

A linked stitch, as its name implies, is one attached to another stitch. It is most often worked over double crochet or longer stitches, but it is possible to link single stitches too. The fabric is not as loose as that made entirely in double crochet, but it will still have a soft drape.

To work a linked double crochet, insert the hook into the side of the post of the previous stitch. You will see a slightly slanting strand of yarn across the middle, this is where to insert the hook. Take the yarn over the hook and draw it through the side of the post. With two loops on the hook, complete the stitch as for a normal double crochet. The stitch will be connected to the middle and top of the previous stitch.

For stitches longer than double crochet, you can either link them into one slanting bar or into each of them. You can also link every stitch or you can link groups, working the others in the usual way.

Question 49:
Which stitch do I use to make a plain fabric?

All of the basic stitches can be used to make a very acceptable piece of crochet. For a firm, dense fabric, use single crochet for every row. If you want something a little softer, with more drape, then use one of the longer stitches, such as double crochet.

Combining the two stitches, one row single crochet with one row double crochet, will give a slightly different texture with a density and drape somewhere between the two. Alternatively, work the first stitch as a single crochet and the second as a double. On the next row, work a double on the single and vice versa.

You can combine the basic stitches in a number of ways to make an easily worked fabric with an interesting texture.

Although all crochet stitches have a degree of texture, if you prefer a smoother fabric, one that more closely resembles the plain side of knitting, work single crochet into the gaps between each stitch rather than into the loops at the top of the stitch. You can also try working into the front loops only, which will make your fabric a little more elastic.

BELOW A half row of single crochet.

Question 50:
Why do the loops fall off the hook?

The loops falling off the hook is a fairly common problem when you start to crochet but one that is easily solved by tightening the tension on the yarn as it is fed to the hook. If you are having this problem, a useful method is to wrap the yarn more times around your little finger or to wrap it around more than one finger. Alternatively, you could try resting the middle finger of your right hand on top of the loop before inserting the hook into the next stitch. Doing this will help you to hold the loop in place while you maneuver the hook.

You will find, however, that the problem of dropped loops is solved of its own accord as you become more familiar with the movements of working the crochet hook and begin to build up a regular rhythm. The yarn will flow from the ball more evenly, and you will automatically achieve smaller loops.

BELOW Wrap the yarn twice around the little finger to give a tighter tension.

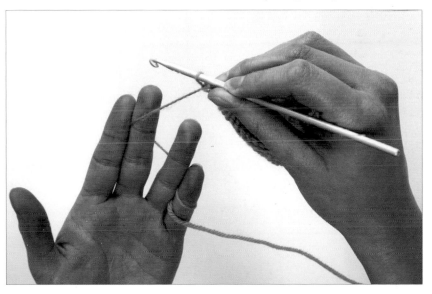

Question 51:
Why can't I draw the yarn through the stitch?

This is the opposite of the previous problem. The answer this time is that you probably have too much tension on the yarn. Your stitches have become so small and tight that, although you could force the point through, it is difficult to draw the hook back with the yarn.

One reason could be that the ball you are working from has wrapped itself around something and the result is that the yarn is not flowing smoothly. Try putting it into a container to stop it rolling around or, where you can, take the yarn from the center of the ball instead of the outside.

Another common fault is splitting the yarn. This is especially easy to do when you are working with loosely spun yarns or ones made up of several strands. If neither of these are the reason your stitches are tight, try holding the yarn in a different way. Let it lie across your palm rather than wrapping it around your little finger. Keep your hands cool and dry. Sprinkle them with talcum powder, which has the added advantage of making your work smell sweet!

Question 52:
Why are my stitches uneven?

The foundation chain is the most difficult part to keep even, as you constantly move your finger and thumb along the chain to get closer to the hook. The chains will even themselves out as you get more comfortable with the technique.

Other uneven stitches are a different matter. Are you working the stitch in the same way each time? Do you always insert the hook from front to back and wrap the yarn from back to front? The first movement of the hook is only to draw it back through the stitch and not to take it through the loop(s) on the hook. Check you have passed the hook under the same strand(s) of the stitch each time. If you are working under two strands in the usual way, make sure that you haven't just picked up one by mistake.

Question 53:
Why do I have too many stitches?

When you are working one of the basic stitches, it is easy to mistake the position of the first and last stitches in a row. After you have worked the required number of turning chains, and before you work the next stitch, look closely at your work. You will see that the turning chain is formed on top of the last stitch of the previous row.

In other words, it stands instead of this stitch for the row you are about to work. So don't work into the stitch directly below the turning chain. Work your next stitch into the following stitch, that is, the second one from the hook.

When you get to the end of a row, look again at your work. You will see that the last stitch looks slightly different than the others. This is because the last stitch was the turning chain of the previous row and was made up of a number of chains. You must work into the top chain of this set in order to obtain the correct number of stitches in the row. The turning chain is counted as a stitch. If you always turn your work in the same direction each time, it will keep the turning chain standard, making it easier to find the correct place to insert the hook.

However, there are some instances where a pattern will instruct you not to count the turning chain as a stitch. Where this is the case, work your last stitch into the top of the first true stitch of the previous row and not into the turning chain at the end. Turn your work, make your turning chain and then work the first stitch into the top of what was your last stitch of the previous row. Remember not to account for the turning chains when you are measuring your work. These turning chains will form a series of loops along the side of the work but will be taken into the side seams when you sew them together.

LEFT The turning chains at the start of each row give a wavy edge to the work which can be hidden in the seams.

Question 54:
How do I join in new yarn?

If you run out of yarn, there are various ways of joining in a new one.

1st method Leaving a tail end of 2 or 3 inches (5–7 cm) of the old yarn, lay it along the wrong side of the work, which may or may not be facing you. Insert the hook into the next stitch, place the new yarn into the hook and draw it through. Insert the hook into the following stitch, under the old strand. Make the next stage of the stitch with both strands of the new yarn, the tail end and the piece that runs from the ball. Work the stitch, covering the old strand at the same time. Complete the row with one strand of the new yarn, working over the old strand each time until it is covered. On the next row, work over the tail end of the new yarn, in the other direction but holding it on the wrong side of the work.

2nd method Again, leave a tail end of the old yarn. Make a slipknot of the new yarn, and place it into the hook before inserting the hook into the next stitch. Hold the strands of both yarns on the wrong side of the work and complete the row, working over both strands of yarn.

RIGHT Two stages of joining in new yarn.

3rd method You can splice some yarns together. Untwist the ends of the old yarn so you can see how many are plied together; do the same with the new yarn. Break off threads from each so you end up with the same number as in the original yarn. Lay the ends, head to tail, and rub them together, moistening your fingers to join them.

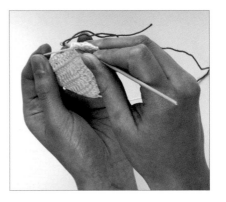

Work carefully so they don't unravel. This method works best for wool and similar hairy yarns but is not so successful with cotton or linen. However, it is sometimes necessary to use this method when working a very lacy pattern, where you don't have a solid row of stitches.

LEFT Splicing yarn.

Question 55:
Do I have to turn the work at the end of each row?

Some crochet stitches have a smoother appearance on one side than the other. There may be times when you don't like the texture that you get when working back and forth in rows. If you want to work with the same side facing you each time, you can either work in rounds or break off the yarn at the end of each row and rejoin it again at the beginning. The first method is useful for hats and sweaters but not so good for flat pieces unless you want them to have a double thickness. The second method also leaves lots of ends that have to be darned in when you finish.

Whichever method you choose, if you are working into the two loops at the top of the stitch, as normal, because they are angled

slightly downward, you will need to insert the hook from below them. This is just a little more awkward than the usual way of working, but it will become easier with practice.

If it is easier, you could also try working into the front or back loops only, always working from right to left and breaking off and rejoining the yarn for each new row.

4
DECORATIVE STITCHES

You can enhance your basic stitches with patterns and embellishments that will turn your piece of crochet into a work of beauty.

Question 56:
How do I make shells?

There are a number of variations on the shell pattern. As you would expect, they create an effect that resembles shells within your crochet work but are all worked in virtually the same way. After making a length of chain stitches, several long stitches are worked into one of them and then a number of chains are missed before working a single crochet or another shell.

Shells can be worked above one another or interlocked by working them into the space between each shell. The latter method of working is illustrated and makes a less-open fabric.

RIGHT Interlocking shells.

HOW IT'S DONE

Make a foundation chain that is a multiple of 6 stitches plus 3.

1 1sc into 2nd ch, *miss 2ch, 5dc in next ch, miss 2ch, 1sc in next ch; rep from * to the end of the row, turn.

2 3ch, 2dc in 1st st, *miss 2dc, 1sc in center dc, miss 2dc, 5dc in sc; rep from *ending with shell, (i.e., 3dc) in last sc, turn.

3 1ch, 1sc in 1st dc, *miss 2dc, 5dc in sc, miss 2dc, 1sc in center dc; rep from * ending with 1sc in top of turning chain, turn.

4 Repeat rows 2 and 3.

You can make shells of more or less than 5 dcs, but you have to miss a corresponding number of chains between them to keep the number of stitches the same.

Question 57:
How do I make picots?

Picots are useful little stitches that can add a more decorative edge to your crochet work, something that often comes in very useful when you are working on a neckline or a child's jacket. They are also used in various mesh stitches. They are especially popular in Irish crochet, where they fill in some of the gaps. They are usually made from three chain stitches, although there is no reason why you can't make larger ones.

RIGHT Three chain picots with three single crochet between each of them.

HOW IT'S DONE

To make a 3-chain picot along an edge:

1 Work 2 or 3sc into the edge or into a row of plain crochet.

2 Make 3ch.

3 Twist the hook back on itself and insert it from right to left into the 3rd chain from the hook.

4 Take the yarn over the hook and draw it back through the stitch and the loop on the hook

5 That makes 1 picot.

6 To complete the edging, work 2 or 3 more single crochet and then make another picot. Repeat to the end of the row.

The same movements are required when making picots on a mesh except that instead of single crochet stitches, you will have worked a number of chains. Make sure that you always insert the hook into the third chain from the hook if you want all your picots to be the same size.

Question 58:
How do I make clusters?

Clusters look similar to upside-down shells. They can be used in conjunction with shells to form flowerlike patterns in your work. They are made by working a number of stitches into each stitch of the previous row, say five, and then gathering them together at the top in a similar way to decreasing. Work four or five chain stitches, and then work another cluster.

BELOW A row of clusters topped with a row of shells.

HOW IT'S DONE

To make one cluster of five double crochet stitches:

1 Yarn over hook and insert it into the next stitch, yarn over again and draw through the stitch, yarn over again and draw through 2 loops on the hook.

2 Yarn over hook and insert it into the next stitch. Continue as above until you have 3 loops on the hook.

3 Repeat these steps 3 more times, until you have 6 loops on the hook.

4 Yarn over hook and draw it through all 6 loops.

5 Make 1 chain. This completes one cluster.

If you are working clusters all along the row, you will need to make a number of chains between them to compensate for the stitches you have lost by gathering them together, which will be 4 chains here, the 5th one being at the top of the cluster.

Question 59:
How do I make bobbles?

Bobbles are similar to clusters. However, the group of stitches are all worked into one stitch, as for making shells, rather than into consecutive stitches as in clusters. The group of stitches are then gathered together at the top as for clusters. Because the number of stitches are being increased from one stitch, there is no need to add extra chain stitches between bobbles. They can be worked next to each other all along the row. They stand out more on the wrong side. As you can imagine, they produce a fabric with a lumpy texture if they are worked all over.

BELOW Two rows of bobbles with a row of double crochet between them.

Like clusters, each stitch is partially made and then the hook is passed through all the loops.

HOW IT'S DONE
To make a 5-stitch bobble in double crochet:

1 Work 5 partial double crochet into one stitch of the previous row.

2 When you have 6 loops on the hook, draw the yarn back through all 6.

You can work another row of bobble stitches into the tops of these, or you can work one or two rows between them. A couple of rows of bobbles worked at the top and bottom of an afghan will give it some weight and help it to hang nicely.

Question 60:
How do I make puffs?

Puffs are patterns within your work that are made into one stitch, like bobbles. They work like popcorn stitches in that they are multiple stitches connected at the top and bottom. However, this time you don't work a partial stitch but simply draw up a series of long loops before fastening them off. In effect, you are making half double crochet stitches but with long strands. This creates a denser effect that stands out within the pattern and gives it texture and depth.

RIGHT Column of puff stitches.

HOW IT'S DONE

To work one puff stitch of 5 strands:

1 Yarn over hook and insert the hook into the next stitch, yarn over hook again and pull on the yarn slightly to draw a long loop through, giving 3 loops on the hook.

2 Repeat these steps until you have 6 long loops on the hook.

3 Yarn over hook and draw through all 6 loops.

4 Make 1chain stitch to fasten off the top of the puff.

5 Just as when you are making bobbles, there is no need to make extra chains between the stitches. They can be made side by side all along the row and over a number of rows.

When they are worked into the gaps between them on succeeding rows, puffs give a soft, springy fabric that is ideal for working with blankets, especially for cribs and strollers.

Question 61:
How do I make popcorns?

Popcorns are similar to bobbles, but they stand out even more because they are folded back on themselves. They can be made over any number of stitches, as can the other stitches just described. They are best made with double crochet or longer stitches. Popcorn stitches give depth and texture to your work.

RIGHT A column of popcorn stitches

HOW IT'S DONE

To make a double crochet popcorn of 5 stitches:

1 Make 5 complete double crochet into one stitch.

2 Take the hook out of the loop that is on it, being careful not to lose the loop, and insert the hook from the front to the back into the top of the first stitch of this group.

3 Insert the hook back into the loop that you took off and draw this loop through the strands on the hook. This popcorn will stand up on the front of the work.

4 If you want the popcorn to recede to the back, work as far as finishing the 5 double crochet.

5 Take the hook out of the loop and insert it from back to front into the first stitch of the group.

6 Insert the hook back into the loop and draw it through the strands on the hook. You can work an extra chain here to fasten off the popcorn securely.

All of these clustered stitches can be worked all over to give a chunky texture to the fabric, or they can be worked in panels to form patterns similar to that of the blackberry stitch in knitting.

Question 62:
How do I make bullions?

Bullions are attractive textural stitches that are especially effective for making flowers or adding bulk to motifs in Irish crochet. This is also sometimes known as the roll stitch.

The actual construction of the bullion stitch is simple. Holding onto the yarn wraps as you try to draw the hook through them all is tricky. The stitch consists of coils of wraps around the hook, through which the yarn is drawn. It's a more difficult technique than most others.

RIGHT Bullions in gray yarn within crochet work.

HOW IT'S DONE

To make 1 bullion stitch:

1 Wrap the yarn around the hook several times, anything between 7 and 12, although 10 is the usual number.

2 Insert the hook into the required stitch and draw a loop through.

3 Wrap the yarn around the hook again and draw it back through all the wraps on the hook.

4 You may find it simpler to pick each strand of yarn with your finger and thumb and lift it over the point of the hook. Take care not to let the next wrap slip off as you do this.

5 Make 1 chain to fasten off the stitch.

6 A wooden hook will often hold the stitches better than a metal or plastic one, especially when you are using a slippery yarn.

You can make bullions in successive stitches or work a number of chains between them, depending on the effect you want to achieve.

Question 63:
How do I make spikes?

Spikes are made in the same way as the basic stitches, but the hook is inserted into a stitch several rows below the one you are working. You need to draw up a loop long enough to reach the base of the row you wish to work into before making the stitch. It needs to be long enough not to squash the earlier rows but not so long that it will get easily snagged. Several spike stitches can be made into one stitch, as for shells, or they can be worked singly, side by side. They are most effective when several rows are worked in a different color and the spikes of one color are made over some of the contrasting rows.

HOW IT'S DONE

To work a series of spikes of graduating height:

1 Work 5 rows of single crochet in color A.

2 Change to color B and work 5 scs.

3 Work a spike over the next stitch, still using color B, which is done by inserting the hook into the next stitch but 3 rows below the one you are working.

4 Draw up a long loop, yarn over hook and draw it through the loop.

5 Insert the hook into the next stitch 2 rows below and make the next spike.

6 Insert the hook into the next stitch 1 row below and make the next spike.

7 Work 3sc.

Repeat this sequence to the end of the row and then work 5 more rows of single crochet in color B. Work the sequence again with color A or with a third color.

LEFT Spikes worked in contrasting colors.

Question 64:
How do I make crossed stitches?

Crochet stitches, especially the longer ones, can be made to cross over each other for an even more intricate, impressive effect. They can either pass in front and behind each stitch, or they can be interlinked.

RIGHT A series of crossed stitches.

HOW IT'S DONE

To do the simplest crossover:
1 Insert the hook into the 3rd stitch and work 1 double crochet, then wrap the yarn around the hook, take the hook behind the stitch just made and insert it from front to back into the 2nd stitch to work the next double crochet.

2 To link the stitches:

Miss 1 stitch and work a double crochet.

Yarn over hook and insert it into the stitch that you missed.

Because the yarn passes behind the first stitch, it will sandwich between the strands of the second one.

You can also make a "Y" shape with longer stitches:
1 Work a double triple and then make 3 or 4 chains.

2 Work a double crochet into the central strand of the double triple.

To make an upside-down "Y" shape starting with 6 chains:
1 Make an uncompleted triple into the 3rd stitch. You will have 3 loops on the hook.

2 Miss 2 stitches and make an uncompleted dc. You will now have 4 loops on the hook.

3 Wrap the yarn again and draw it through 2 loops.

4 Repeat this step twice more until you have 1 loop left.

5 Make 3 chains to take you on to the next stitch.

Question 65:
How do I make loop stitches?

Loop stitch, or fur stitch, as its name implies, forms a series of loops on the side of the work facing away from you. It is made in the same way as single crochet, but long loops of yarn are caught with the index or middle finger before finishing off the stitch.

HOW IT'S DONE

1 Begin by working a row of single crochet.

2 Turn, work 1 single crochet, and then insert your hook into the next stitch.

3 With the yarn over your finger, hold it up high and catch the base of the strand at the back of your finger, draw it through the stitch.

4 Catch the base of the back strand again and draw it through the 2 loops.

5 Take your finger out of the loop and insert the hook into the next stitch, ready to repeat the process.

6 Unless you want loops to appear on both sides of your work, make the next row from basic stitches, singles or doubles, and then work the loop row again.

7 The loops can be cut, they won't pull out, to make a more furry-looking piece, especially luxurious when worked in a mohair yarn.

8 If you are going to be joining the pieces, keep 1 or 2 stitches at the edges without loops.

ABOVE Holding yarn on middle finger to form a loop on the wrong side.

BELOW Finished piece of loopy crochet.

Question 66:
How do I make spiders?

Spiders are patterns within the crochet work that spread out from a central point in multiple directions, much like the legs of a spider. These embellishments are made from a mixture of chains and triples. They can be worked all over your piece of crochet if you want to form a very open pattern, or they can be used individually as accents.

RIGHT Two blocks of spiders.

HOW IT'S DONE

To make an allover pattern:

1 Begin with a foundation chain that is a multiple of 18 plus 8.

2 1dc into 8th ch, *2ch, miss 2ch, 1dc into next ch; rep from * to end, turn.

3 5ch, 1dc into next dc, *4ch, 1tr into each of next 4dc, 4ch, 1dc in next dc, 2ch, 1dc in next dc; rep from * to end, working last dc into 3rd ch of turning ch, turn.

4 5ch, 1dc into next dc, *4ch, 1sc into each of next 4tr, 4ch, 1dc into next dc, 2ch, 1dc in next dc; rep from * to end, turn.

5 5ch, 1dc into next dc, *4ch, 1sc into each of next 4sc, 4ch, 1dc in next dc, 2ch, 1dc in next dc; rep from * to end, turn.

6 Repeat row 4.

7 5ch, 1dc in next dc, *2ch, (1tr in next sc, 2ch) 4 times, 1dc in next dc, 2ch, 1dc in next dc; rep from * to end, turn.

8 5ch, 1dc in next dc, *2ch (1dc in next tr, 2ch) 4 times, 1dc in next dc, 2ch, 1dc in next dc; rep from * to end, turn.

9 Rows 2 to 7 form the spiders. Either repeat them, or work row 1 again one or more times between each row of spiders.

Question 67:
How do I make fans?

Fans are very similar to shells in appearance and they are also worked in the same way, making a number of stitches into the same place. Like shells, they can be worked in long stitches over one row, but unlike shells, fans can also take more than one row to complete. They are often based on a row of chain arches in order to make them fan out more. They can also be decorated with picots, as in the following pattern.

BELOW **Fan** edged with picots.

Question 68:
How do I make Catherine wheels?

Catherine wheels make very attractive allover patterns. They look complex but are really very simple to work, being made up of alternate rows of clusters and fans or shells, separated by chain stitches. They are solid enough for jackets, purses or afghans but still soft enough to give some fluidity to the fabric. Stitching a Catherine wheel takes longer than most other crochet stitches and patterns, but the thick and intricate effect is worth the effort. The Catherine wheel can appear either as a gothic marigold or as a circular, spinning firework shape, where the radiating spines of the wheel resemble spokes.

The beauty of the Catherine wheel stitch is that it gives you the potential to use two different yarns while giving each the potential to develop its own strength and show off its color without one dissolving into the other. This makes it useful for decorative items like scarves. Pieces can be made in one or more colors as shown in the

BELOW Bicolored Catherine wheels.

sample, which is worked using blue and white over two rows each. An interesting effect can be obtained with one solid color and one variegated one, changing over on rows two and four as before. To give an even softer drape, use one of the longer triple stitches in place of the double crochet.

EXPERT TIP

❝ Catherine wheels can also be used to make an attractive braid. Make as many chains as you need for the length required and then work rows 1-6 as below. Work the first two rows in main color then 3 rows in contrast, then 2 rows in the main color again. ❞

HOW IT'S DONE

Make a foundation chain that is a multiple of 10 plus 7 stitches.

1 1sc in 2nd ch, sc in next ch, *miss 3ch, 7dc in next ch, miss 3ch, sc in each of next 3ch, rep from * to last 4ch, miss 3ch, 4dc in last ch, turn.

2 1ch, sc in each of next 2st, *3ch, 7st cluster, 3ch, sc in each of next 3st; rep from * to last 4, 3ch, 4st cluster, turn.

3 3ch, 3dc in 1st st, *miss ch space, 1sc in each of next 3sc, miss next ch space, 7dc in top of cluster; rep from * to end, miss last ch space, 1sc in each of next 2sc, turn.

4 3ch, miss 1st st, 3st cluster, *3ch, 1sc in each of next 3st, 3ch, 7st cluster; rep from * to end, 3ch, 1sc in last st, 1sc in tch, turn.

5 1ch, 1sc in each of next 2sc, *miss ch space, 7dc in top of cluster, miss next ch space, 1sc in each of next 3sc; rep from * to end, miss last ch space, 4dc in top of tch, turn.

6 Rows 2 to 4 form the Catherine wheels.

If you work rows 2 and 3 in the first color and 4 and 5 in the second color, the Catherine wheels will stand out as circles.

Question 69:
How do I make a trellis pattern?

Trellis patterns are the simplest and quickest way to make a large piece of crochet if you are in need of a large item and are not especially bothered about its appearance. This is because they are not particularly decorative. However, the speed with which you can crochet them makes them ideal for making anything that is open and meshlike, such as string bags.

Trellis patterns are made up of chains forming a series of arches and single crochet stitches worked into the arches. There can be any number of chains to the arch, but the usual number is five.

RIGHT A trellis stitch.

HOW IT'S DONE

To begin a 5-chain trellis, make a foundation chain that is a multiple of 4 stitches plus 6.

1 1sc into 6th chain from hook, *5ch, miss 3ch, 1sc into next ch; rep from * to end.

2 Turn.

3 *5ch, 1sc into the arch; rep from * to end, turn.

4 Repeat the 2nd row.

Arches can also be interspersed with other stitches within your pattern. For example, shells or blocks of double crochet could be worked into alternate arches on right-side rows.

You might also decide to create a pattern that has picots worked over the single crochets, as in an Irish crochet mesh.

Question 70:
How do I make love knots?

The love knot, also known as Soloman's knot, looks as though it ought to be quite complicated. It is actually just a series of long loops fastened together with a single crochet. It takes some practice to get all of the loops of an equal size. Once you have mastered this, you will find it a useful and versatile stitch. It is a very open stitch, ideal for making shawls and shrugs as well as lacy scarves. It is especially attractive when worked in a fine mohair.

The knot is formed in stages so that the stitch forms a diamond-shaped mesh. The lower half of the diamond is worked first, and then the upper half is worked on the following row.

RIGHT Love knot.

HOW IT'S DONE

To make one love knot:

1 After making a slipknot, work 1ch, pulling the loop to lengthen it to approximately ¼ to ½ inch (½–1 cm).

2 Wrap the yarn over the hook and draw it through the loop to its normal length. There will be 3 long strands coming from the initial slipknot.

3 Insert the hook under the last loop made, the single one, wrap the yarn over again and draw it through both loops to make 1sc and complete 1 knot.

4 Make a foundation row of a multiple of 2 of these knots.

5 Make knots into alternate single crochet stitches between the long loops, making these loops a little longer than those for the foundation row, turn.

6 Make 2 short love knots for the edge of the work, and then complete the row with longer ones as for the first row.

7 Repeat row 2 for allover knots.

Question 71:
What are pineapples?

Pineapples are lacy stitches formed from a number of rows of short arches, which are in turn divided by chains and double crochets to make them stand out. They are in very popular patterns for household items of all kinds and lend themselves particularly to circular pieces.

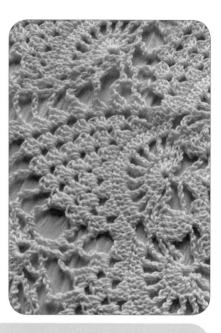

The pattern below is for a small pineapple worked over five double crochet and taking four rows to complete. However, any number of double crochet can be worked here. The more there are, the more rows of arches it will take to complete the pineapple.

RIGHT Rows of pineapples.

HOW IT'S DONE

1 Make a multiple of 12 chains plus 3. 1sc in 2nd ch, *3ch, in 6th ch work (1dc, 1ch) 4 times, 1dc in same place, 3ch, 1sc in 6th ch; rep from * 1sc in last stitch, turn.

2 3ch, 1dc in 1st stitch, *1ch, miss 1st ch space (1sc in ch space, 3ch) 3 times, 1sc in last ch space 1ch, (2dc, 1ch, 2dc) all into sc; rep from *, ending with 1ch, 2dc in last sc, turn.

3 3ch, 1dc in 1st dc, * 2ch, (1sc in 3ch arch, 3ch) twice, 1sc in last arch, 2ch, (2dc, 1ch, 2dc) all into ch space between pairs of dc; rep from *, ending with 2ch, 2dc in last stitch, turn.

4 3ch, 1dc in 1st stitch, of dc, *3ch, 1sc in arch 3ch, 1sc in next arch, 3ch, (2dc, 1ch, 2dc) all into ch space bet pairs of dc; rep from *, ending with 3ch, 2dc in last stitch, 1ch, turn.

Repeat these 4 rows to make a series of pineapples, working the base of each new pineapple into the arch at the head of the previous one and working the single crochet between the pairs of double crochet.

Question 72:
How do I make slanting blocks?

There are all kinds of block patterns, which can be used to make simple but beautiful pieces. The basic blocks are made of a number of double crochet stitches worked into the corresponding number of chains or chain spaces.

However, these normally upright blocks can be made to slant right or left by working them into the side of a double crochet or into a 3-chain space worked alongside the block.

An attractive pattern is made by inserting a "V" stitch between the slanting blocks, as is described in the box to the right.

HOW IT'S DONE

To make a slanting block pattern, make a foundation chain that is a multiple of 10 plus 4.

1 1dc in 4th ch, *3ch, miss 4ch, 1sc in next, 3ch, 3dc in same ch, miss 4ch, (1dc, 1ch, 1dc) all into 5th ch, rep from *, ending 2dc in last ch, turn.

2 3ch, 1dc in 1st dc, *3ch, 1sc in top of 3ch, 3ch, 1dc in side of 3ch of previous row, (1dc, 1ch, 1dc) in ch sp bet dcs; rep from * ending 2dc in tch, turn, 3ch.

3 Repeat row 2 for the pattern.

BELOW Rows of slanting blocks separated by "V" stitches.

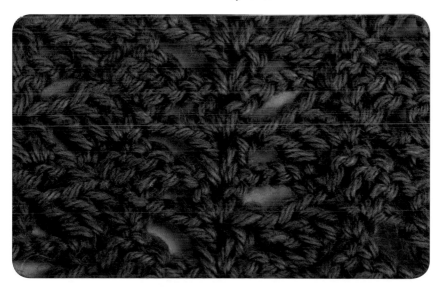

5
EDGINGS, INSERTS AND BRAIDS

Complete your crochet work with decorative touches, inserting them into your pattern, attaching them to the edges or creating braids to complement the flow of the work.

Question 73:
What is the difference between edgings, inserts and braids?

These terms refer to trimmings or decorative edges on a finished piece. Edgings can be worked directly on the piece or stitched on afterward. If they are to be crocheted directly onto the fabric, they are made horizontally and worked into the stitches at the top or bottom, or along the sides. They can be of any depth and usually finish with a scalloped or zigzag edge. Edgings can also be made vertically, where they will usually have one straight edge and one more-decorative one.

Inserts and braids are worked independently of the main fabric and attached afterward. Inserts most often have two straight edges and are placed between two sections of fabric, with no fabric behind them.

Braids are more akin to edgings but are not usually very deep. They are frequently made vertically rather than horizontally. The simplest braid is formed from a series of shells worked along one side of a foundation row, which is then turned so that a second row can be worked to match along the other side. Braids

can be used on the edges of other pieces or twisted into other shapes and applied on top.

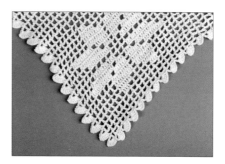

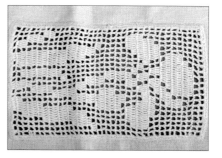

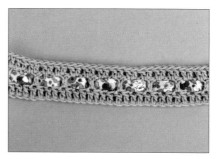

RIGHT Examples of a crochet edging, crochet insert and crochet braid.

Question 74:
What are the uses of edgings, inserts and braids?

These crochet trims can be used to personalize all sorts of plain items. Edgings look especially luxurious on household linens and towels. An edging with a matching insert can enhance a plain tablecloth. An insert could also be used to replace part of a fabric that may have become stained or worn.

Braids can transform a plain T-shirt or be used with matching fringe or tassels to decorate a cushion, curtains or even a lampshade. They can also be stitched to a purse, with beads or buttons added as highlights.

A more functional use is to lengthen children's garments. If you add an edging to clothing in this way, make sure it will wash the same as the main fabric. Another use of edging is as a detachable collar. Either make a straight piece and gather it onto the neckline of a plain sweater or, if you are more ambitious, shape the neck edge and fasten the front edges with a brooch.

Question 75:
How do I attach an edging to a piece of linen?

If the fabric is loosely woven, the neatest way to attach an edging is first to work a row of single crochet into the fabric, using a small, sharp hook. Fold a small hem to the wrong side and tack it. If it is hard to pierce the fabric with the hook, prick the holes with a darning needle. Space the stitches evenly so the edging will lie flat, and work the first row of the edging directly into these stitches.

If the fabric is too closely woven to work into directly, embroider a series of buttonhole stitches around the edge, as close as possible in size to the crochet stitches. Work your first row into these stitches. To attach an edging worked vertically, tack it in place and oversew it neatly to the fabric with a matching thread. Where it is attached to a raw edge, turn under and hem stitch that too.

Question 76:
How do I attach an insert to a piece of linen?

When you have made your insert, block and press it to the required size and shape. Leave to dry if you have steamed or dampened it. When it is ready, place it right side up on the linen. Tack it in place and then, with a fine matching thread and sharp needle, stitch it to the fabric by oversewing the outer edge, spacing the stitches fairly close together. Remove the tacking stitches. Turn the work over and cut away the fabric from behind the insert, leaving ¼ to ½ inch (½–1 cm) of fabric at the edges. Turn under these raw edges and slip stitch them neatly in place, making sure that the stitches don't come through to the crochet.

Question 77:
How do I make a ribbed edging for a crocheted sweater?

There are a number of ways to make edges that resemble ribbing. They will be a little more elastic than normal crochet but not as elastic as a knitted edge. The first method is to work around the posts of double crochet. Work the foundation chain and then a row of double crochet. Into this row, work one double crochet around the front post of the first stitch and one double crochet around the back post of the next stitch. Repeat all along the row. On the second row, work around the back of the post you previously worked around the front of and vice versa. You could also work these stitches in pairs so that the stitches resemble a K2 P2 rib.

The second method is to work a piece horizontally and then pick up stitches along the edge of it to complete the garment.

Make a short length of chain, about 2 inches (5 cm) wide, and work a single crochet into each stitch. On the next row, work into only the back loop of each stitch and repeat this row until the work is long enough.

Question 78:
How do I make a picot edging?

There are a number of ways of finishing an edge with picots. They make attractive edgings for baby clothes or for the necklines of an otherwise plain sweater as well as a decorative finish for afghans and blankets made from motifs. They are also frequently used in Irish crochet to form a more ornate mesh.

The picots themselves are made from chain loops, which can comprise any number of chains but usually three. These chains are then closed into a circle by making a slip stitch into the first of them, as described on page 132.

BELOW Simple picots along the top, arched picots along the side edge.

HOW IT'S DONE

1 Work 1 single crochet into the first two stitches, make 1 picot, miss 1 stitch, work 2 or 3 more single crochet.

2 Make another picot and so on along the row, finishing with 1 single crochet into the last stitch.

3 A more-open picot edge can be made by forming a series of chain arches with picots at their center.

4 Work 1 row of sc into the edge, turn.

5 1ch, 1sc into the first stitch.

6 *Make 6ch, 1ss into the 3rd chain from the hook, make 4ch, miss 2 stitches.

7 Work 1sc into the next stitch. Repeat from * to the end.

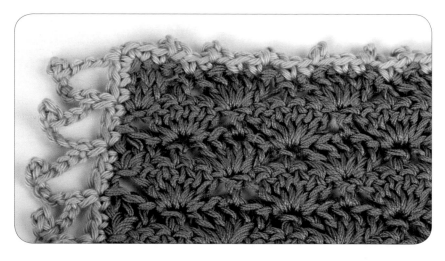

Question 79:
How do I make a shell edging?

A shell edging is slightly more obvious than a picot edging, although no less decorative. A row of shells makes an attractive finish to a plain or multicolored piece of work such as a patchwork throw, or it can be used to trim a plain knitted item rather than working a ribbed band. Use a hook one or two sizes smaller than the needles or hook used for the main piece.

There are several versions of shell edgings. They can be worked directly onto the edge of the piece or into a row of single crochet that has been worked first.

BELOW A shell edging on a piece of work.

HOW IT'S DONE

To work an edging of 5 stitch shells:

1 Work a row of single crochet into the edge and then turn.

2 Work 3ch, *2dc into the same stitch, miss 2sts, work 1sc into the next st, miss 2sts, work 5dc into the next st; rep from * to end, ending with 3dc in the last st.

3 If you want to turn a corner, work two shells with 1sc between them into the same corner stitch.

4 For a more rounded shell, work the stitches of graduating height. For example:

1sc, 1hdc, 1dc, 1tr, 1dc, 1hdc, 1sc all into the same stitch.

Question 80:
What is the crab stitch?

Crab stitch, also known as the reverse single crochet or the corded edge, gives a neat finish to an edge that resembles cording – hence its alternative name.

It is made by working single crochet in the opposite direction to normal, that is, from left to right. It can feel slightly awkward to work this way at first as the hook has to be twisted slightly toward you.

HOW IT'S DONE

To work the crab stitch:

1 With the right side of the work facing you, insert the hook from front to back, into the stitch immediately to the right of the last one.

2 Point the hook slightly downward and catch the yarn at the back.

3 Bring the yarn through the stitch.

4 Wrap the yarn over the hook and draw it through the 2 loops.

5 Repeat to the end of the row and fasten off.

The crab stitch is always worked in single crochet and is intended to be a shallow edging.

LEFT An edging of crab stitch on a slanting blocks pattern.

Question 81:
How do I work an edging around a neckline?

Crochet is not as elastic as knitting, so don't make your neck edging too tight. Don't make it too loose either, or it will not lie flat and may roll back. Use a hook one or two sizes smaller than for the main body. After joining the shoulder seams, starting at the right-hand edge of the back neck, work one single crochet into each stitch along the back.

Assuming you have worked the main piece in short stitches, such as single crochet, work one single crochet into each row end down the left front neck, one into each stitch along the front, and one into each stitch up the right side of the neck.

If your main piece is worked in stitches longer than single crochet, work a compensatory number of single crochet into the row ends of the left and right front neck edges. For example, if you have worked in the equivalent of a double crochet stitch, work two single crochets into each row end along the left neck, one into the head of each stitch of the front neck, and two into each row end of the right neck. This single row can complete your neck edging. However, it is more usual to work a few more rounds of single crochet or a round of a more decorative edging.

Question 82:
How do I turn the corners?

If you are edging a simple round neck, there is no need to accommodate the corners. Where you have a shaped neck or one that is square, U or V, you will need to decrease at the turns. This is done by working two stitches together.

When you are trimming such items as tablecloths, you can either work extra stitches into the corner stitch, forming a series of gathers at that point, or work part rows. From the outside edge, work across two or three stitches, then turn and work back. On the next row, work across these stitches, plus two or three more, turn and work back. Repeat this procedure until you have worked all the stitches back to the corner. Either continue on to the next side

section or repeat the procedure in reverse to make a right angle.

Alternatively, each section of the border can be worked separately, leaving some stitches unworked at the end of each row, forming an angle. You will then need to stitch these corners together after the edgings have been joined to the main piece of work.

EXPERT TIP

❝ If you are working all around a blanket, remember to work three stitches into each of the corners so that the edging will turn the corner neatly. ❞

Question 83:
How do I make a more-decorative edging?

There are many patterns for edgings; the variety is virtually infinite. You can make an edging in a different yarn than the one used for the main piece if you want it to be more obvious. It's best to make sure that the type you choose is either the same as, or will wash the same as, the main yarn. Alternatively, you can make the edging detachable.

Whether you are making it in the same yarn or a different one, first work a row of single crochet around the edge, to even out any steps in the shaping.

A simple but attractive frilled edging for the hem or cuffs of a sweater can be made by working increasing numbers of chains between pairs of shells.

BELOW The illustration shows a similar edging but not an exact match to that of the instructions.

HOW IT'S DONE

Begin by working groups of 3dc, 1ch, all along the edge of the piece of material you are edging.

1 5ch, 3dc into 1st st, *1sc in next ch (3dc, 2ch, 3dc) all into next ch; rep from *, ending with 4dc in last st, turn.

2 5ch, 3dc in 1st st, *(1dc, 2ch, 1dc) in next st, (3dc, 2ch, 3dc) in next st; rep from *, ending 4dc in last st, turn.

3 Repeat row 2 twice more and then increase again.

4 5ch, 3dc in 1st st, *(1dc, 2ch, 1dc, 2ch, 1dc) in next st, (3dc, 2ch, 3dc) in next st; rep from * ending with 4dc in last st.

5 Repeat the last row as many times as required, or work other increase rows to make the edging even more full.

Other attractive edgings can be made with filet crochet. Very ornate edgings can be found in the old illustrated magazines such as Ann Orr's *Crochet Designs* or the various publications by the Priscilla Publishing Co. of Boston.

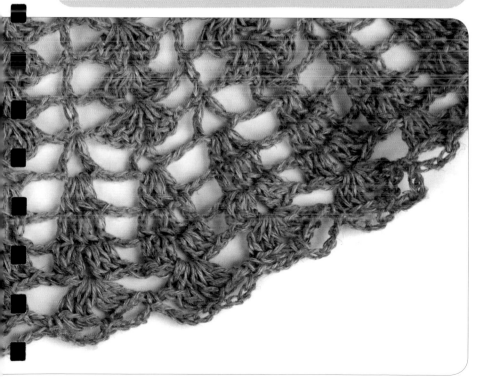

Question 84:
How do I know how many stitches to start with?

This question depends on the type of edging that you have decided to make. If you are making a horizontal edging that is separate from the main fabric and uses a different yarn, it's best to make a gauge swatch first.

Count how many stitches you get to the inch with your edging, and then measure the edge you want to trim. Work out how many chains to make for your foundation row, as described on page 30, according to the pattern as well as your measurements. Remember that foundation chains can often be tighter than the other stitches. If you usually have this problem, try making your foundation chain with a larger hook or working one of the alternative foundation chains as described on page 32. This will make the edging more flexible and easier to attach to the main piece.

If you are working the edge directly onto the fabric, divide the fabric with pins into equal segments. Pick up the same number of stitches between each set of pins. You want the crochet to lie flat and not buckle or pull in, so work out from your gauge swatch the correct number of stitches to work here. If you have the same gauge as your main piece work, work one single crochet for each stitch along a horizontal edge and approximately three stitches for every four single crochet around an inner curve.

Where the main piece is worked in longer stitches, you will have to judge how many single crochet stitches are equivalent to one of the longer ones. The number of turning chains you worked at the beginning of each row is a good guide as one chain is the same width as one single crochet.

Question 85:
How do I make braids?

As with edgings, there are a number of different patterns for braids. They should a have neat edges along both sides as they will be applied on to the top of a piece of fabric. The majority of braids are symmetrical, but this is not compulsory – you can be as creative as you like. They are usually quite narrow and can stand alone or have beads or ribbons added to them.

BELOW Example of a braid threaded with ribbon.

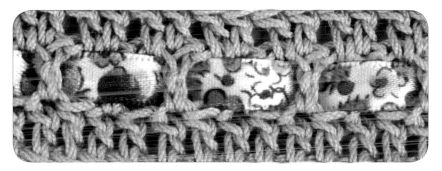

HOW IT'S DONE

A simple lengthwise braid is made by working a series of double crochets into chain spaces:

1 Begin with 8ch, joined into a circle with a ss.

2 3ch, 7dc into circle, 6ch, 1sc into circle, turn.

3 3ch, 7dc into ch space, 6ch, 1sc into ch space, turn.

4 Repeat row 2 for the required length.

5 A braid suitable for threading ribbon through is made by working a foundation chain as long as you want the braid and then working a row of double crochet.

6 Next row, work 1 double crochet, 1 chain, miss a stitch, all along the row. Finish with another row of double crochet.

Weave ribbon in and out between as many of the double crochets as you choose. You could also work a similar braid in triples or longer stitches and use even wider ribbon.

6

SHAPING

Not every piece of crochet you might want to make will be straight at the edges – sleeves, necklines and decoratively edged flat pieces will all need attention to shape.

Question 86:
How do I decrease at the beginning and end of a row?

Exactly how you decrease depends on which stitch you are using. When you are working in single crochet, to decrease at the beginning of a row, make the turning chain but then miss it and insert the hook into the following stitch. At the end of the row, in order to make the edges match, miss the last stitch and work into the top of the turning chain. If

you miss the turning chain, you will get a stepped edge, which is not as easy to join. The same method applies to the basic stitches, but the edge will be neater if you also make one fewer turning chain than usual at the beginning of the rows.

If you are working a shell pattern, work half a shell instead of a full one at the beginning and end of a row. Where there is already only a half shell at each end, slip stitch across the one at the beginning of the row and miss it completely at the end.

BELOW Decreasing showing a gradual slope at the right and a series of small steps on the left.

Question 87:
How do I decrease several stitches together?

If you need to decrease more than two stitches at the beginning of a row in order to shape a piece of work, the easiest method is to use slip stitches. Don't make a turning chain or work into the first stitch. Slip stitch into the number of stitches as stated in the pattern instructions, then make your turning chain and complete the row as set.

At the end of the row, stop at the required number of stitches before you reach the end, remembering that the turning chain is counted as a stitch. Turn, and complete the work as per the instructions. This method of decreasing will leave a series of steps, but these will not be noticeable when the seams are made as they should dovetail into one another.

If you need to decrease three or more stitches together, work the

first part of the stitch as normal as far as the last two loops on the hook. Work the next stitch in the same way, leaving the last 2 loops on the hook.

Continue in this way for each stitch that is to be lost. Finally, take the yarn over the hook and draw it through all of the remaining loops.

Some patterns, especially those of bobbles, clusters and so on, require you to decrease several stitches simultaneously to form the pattern. Full instructions for these were given in Chapter 4.

RIGHT Slip stitch over six stitches at the beginning of the row, six stitches left at the end of the row, and three stitches decreased at each end of the next row.

Question 88:
How do I increase a stitch at the beginning and end of a row?

After forming the turning chain at the beginning of the row, making it just a little looser than normal, work the first stitch into the stitch that this turning chain stands on. At the end of the row, work twice into the turning chain.

This is the easiest and most usual method of increasing a stitch at the beginning or end of the row. However, it can form a bulky and uneven seam, especially when using thicker yarns. You will obtain a smoother edge by working the extra stitch one or two stitches away from the turning chain. Work the turning chain, and then make two stitches into the next stitch.

The seam will be even less bulky if you work the first of these stitches into the back loop and the second stitch into the front loop. Work to the last two stitches, make two stitches into the next stitch, into the front and then the back loop, and finally work one stitch into the turning chain.

Question 89:
How do I increase more than one stitch?

If you are working with single or double crochet, the easiest method of increasing two or three stitches at each end of a row is to work them into one stitch, as above. Work the extra stitches at the beginning of the row into the stitch that the turning chain stands on. At the end of the row, work them all into the top of the turning chain. Make the turning chains a little looser than you normally would.

However, if you are working these increases over more than about six consecutive rows or if you are using longer stitches, the work will start to pull because the stitches are not long enough to accommodate the angle of the slope. You can either increase the length of the turning chain or, better yet, add on extra chains.

Question 90:
How do I increase stitches in the middle of a row?

Increasing in the middle of a row gives a slight curve to the work. This can be used to form waves or zigzags, which will make a decorative theme within the pattern. It is especially useful when it is combined with the corresponding number of stitches decreased. The increases are simply worked by making two or more stitches in the same stitch on the previous row. Don't alternate between back and front loops in this case, however. Work each extra stitch into the top of the stitch of the previous row or into the space between the stitches, depending on the pattern. These multiple mid-row increases are used to form specific patterns and not usually to shape an item, unless you are forming a three-dimensional object or if you are working in the round. To work shapings that will give your piece of crochet some extra width, you can either work two stitches into one or work an extra stitch between existing stitches. The method you use will depend on the stitch pattern and will usually be given in the instructions. If you are working a piece entirely in one of the basic stitches, the simplest way is to work into the space between them.

BELOW Increases and decreases to form a series of waves.

Question 91:
How do I decrease or increase evenly across a row?

To decrease or increase evenly across a row means to space out your changes at regular intervals. If you don't do this, you will have all your added stitches at the beginning of the row, making the item lopsided. To work out how to space them evenly, you need to do some math.

Where it is not stated in the pattern, to decrease evenly you first need to work out how many stitches you must lose by subtracting the new total from the number of stitches currently in the row. When you have the result, divide it into the current number of stitches. Subtract 2 from this number, as these are the stitches that will be worked together and that will give you the number of stitches to work between decreases.

To increase, work out how many stitches you need to add to give the new total. Add 1 to this number for the increased stitch. Next, divide this result into the existing number of stitches and to find the number of stitches to work between the increases.

HOW IT'S DONE

For example, you have 25 stitches and you need to increase this number to 30.

1 This means you need 5 more, so add 5 + 1 = 6.

2 Divide 25 by 6, which gives 4 remainder 1.

3 Add this 1 to 4 in order to work out how many stitches you need at the beginning and end of the row.

4 The answer is 5, which means you work 3 at the beginning and 2 at the end (or vice versa if you prefer) and 4 between each of the other increases.

5 The increases can then either be worked directly into each 4th stitch or between the 4th and following stitch.

If you get a remainder in your final total, add it to the whole number and divide that result by 2. These are the stitches you will work at the beginning and end of the row, with the rest spaced evenly.

Question 92:
How do I maintain the pattern when I start shaping?

This is not such a complex issue as it can be in lace knitting because it is easy to see how the pattern is formed in crochet. If a shell has always been worked into the center of a shell on the previous row, you will continue to do this even where you have decreased some stitches at the beginning or end of the row. The usual method of decreasing shells is to work only a half one at each end.

To decrease this half shell on the following decrease row, slip stitch across to the center of the next shell, work in pattern to the last full shell and stop halfway along it. Turn and work back.

This method of decreasing can be applied to any of the multiple stitch patterns. It gives a series of short steps, but they can be hidden in a wide seam. You can even dovetail them into their counterparts at the top of a sleeve if you are joining the edges with crochet stitches.

BELOW Half shells worked in place of full shells on two rows and 1 double crochet worked into the center of a shell on the top row.

Question 93:
How do I cast on a number of stitches at the beginning of a row?

If you are working a sweater from the top down, you may need to add several stitches at the underarm or at the neck edge of a cardigan. Where you need to increase more than two stitches at the start of a row, you will need to make extra chains as a foundation for the additional stitches. Make one chain for each stitch, plus enough for the turning chain, according to the stitch you are working in. When you have the right number of chains, work the appropriate stitches into them and continue in pattern across the row.

HOW IT'S DONE

For example, to add 5 double crochets at the beginning of a row:

1 Work to the end of preceding row and make 7 chains.

2 Turn and work 1dc into the 4th ch, the first 3ch will stand as your 1st dc.

3 Work 1dc into each of the next 3ch, then continue across the row in pattern to the end.

BELOW Four stitches increased at the beginning of the row, followed by the next pattern row with a half shell.

Question 94:
How do I cast on a number of stitches at the end of a row?

There are two ways to add extra stitches at the end of a row. Both require extra chains, but one means joining on extra yarn. The simplest method is to remove your hook from the loop three or four stitches from the end of the row. Slip a safety pin or stitch marker into it to keep it from pulling back. Join a spare length of yarn to the top of the last stitch and work the required number of chains. Fasten off and return your hook to the loop that you left before continuing to work the last few stitches plus the additional ones into the new length of chain. The alternative method is to work the extra chains and stitches all in one.

HOW IT'S DONE

Alternative method:

1 At the end of the row work 1tr into the last st (the reason you work a tr and not a dc is because you use the bottom of the tr as a mock chain).

2 Yarn around hook and work 1tr into the vertical loop at the base of the first one worked.

3 Yarn around hook and insert the hook into the base of the last one worked.

4 Continue in this way, adding more and more stitches as required.

BELOW Extra chains being worked at side edge while a safety pin holds the "live" stitch.

BELOW Single crochet worked into extra chains (contrast yarn used for clarity).

Question 95:
How do I bind off a number of stitches at the end of a row?

Decreasing a number of stitches at the end of a row is the simplest procedure of all. You simply stop when you have worked the required number of stitches, turn and, after working the appropriate turning chain, work back along the row. Stop again before reaching the end if you are decreasing at both edges of a piece. If you are working fairly long stitches, it may also mean that the decreased stitches at one edge of the garment are ½ inch (1 cm) or more higher up than at the other edge. In this case, you may find it makes a better finish to work slip stitch over the stitches at the beginning of the row that you are stopping before the end.

If you would prefer not to have steps, for instance if you are shaping a neckline and want a smooth curve, then use the method of decreasing several stitches together. If there are too many stitches to decrease all at once into one stitch, work two or more side by side until you have reduced the stitches to the correct number.

BELOW Crochet work that has been stopped before the end of a row and then decreased on the following row.

Question 96:
How do I bind off in the middle of a row?

Binding off in the middle of a row is utilized for shaping necklines or occasionally when working in the round. The simplest method is to work across to where you want the neckline or underarm to start and then leave a number of stitches before turning and working back to the other end.

Continue these stitches only for each row, making any shaping as required. When this section is completed, keeping the right side facing you and leaving the required number of stitches at the center, rejoin the yarn to the next stitch. Then finish the second section as you did the first.

You might be tempted to turn the work and rejoin the yarn at the side edge, but this could leave a distinct change in the pattern. Depending on how many stitches are decreased at the shaped edge, you may be left with a series of steps. This does not matter, as they will usually be hidden when you work the neckband or set in the sleeves.

EXPERT TIP

❝ An alternative way of binding off in the middle of the work, especially where stitches are to be bound off over several rows, is to work to the point where the stitches are to be lost and then work slip stitches over these. Continue in pattern to the end of the row, working a turning chain at the beginning if necessary in order to bring the hook to the required height. On the second row, if more stitches are to be decreased, work the required number of stitches and turn before reaching the end. On the third row, slip stitch across the number of stitches to be bound off again. Repeat these last two rows as many times as instructed. Again, when you rejoin the yarn for the other section, keep the same side of the work facing you. ❞

Question 97:
How do I cast on in the middle of a row?

Casting on in the middle of the row is not a very common occurrence. It can be employed when working garments from the top down, especially those that are worked on a yoke. Stitches often need to be added at the underarms to allow for movement. All you do is work a number of chains between the pattern stitches and then work into them on the following row, just as you would when increasing at the beginning of a row.

For example, after working several rows of the yoke, work across a number of the stitches, leaving enough for the head of the sleeve. Make an equivalent number of chains in their place.

Finish the back and fronts. Then work across the stitches of the back, and do the same for the other sleeve. On the next row, work in pattern across the chains. Pick up the stitches around the gap later to work the sleeves.

BELOW Casting on in the middle of a row.

Question 98:
How do I do raglan shaping?

Raglan shaping is just as simple in crochet as it is in knitting, especially when using one of the basic stitches. Make sure that you know your stitch and row gauge so that you can work out which rows to perform the decreases on. Decreasing at each end of every row will give a shallow angle to the slope. It may be better to work the decreases on every 3rd or 4th row

For a fashionable appearance, work the decreases two or three stitches in from the edge. Unlike knitting stitches, where the stitches are worked together in different ways depending on which end of the row they are, the direction of slope of the decreased crochet stitches will look similar whichever end of the row they are worked on. So there is no need to alter the way you work them.

If you are working a complicated pattern stitch, switch to plain stitches for the edges of the raglans, working the full pattern stitch only where it will next fit along the row.

Question 99:
How do I shape the top of a set-in sleeve?

Set-in sleeves are not always successful in crochet, especially when using a bulky yarn. If you think that the yarn is too thick to work a neat decrease, you could work a modified drop sleeve. This has a straight top but is inset into the body of the garment for 1 inch (2 cm). Bind off 1 inch (2 cm) of stitches at the start of the armhole to accommodate the top on the body of the sleeve. On the sleeve work the length required. Then work enough extra rows to slot into this space and fasten off. Stitch the straight edge of the sleeve head to the armhole edge of the body. Then join sleeve and side seams in one.

With finer yarns, sleeve heads can be shaped as for the armhole on the body. However, with many pattern stitches, this will leave a series of steps along the curve. These steps should be matched as far as possible with their opposite numbers on the body when sewing in the sleeve. They will then form a smoother join and be less noticeable.

Question 100:
How do I shape a neckline?

The easiest neckline to work with when making a crochet garment is a square one. To make one of these, you will need to work across approximately one-third of the stitches, then turn and complete this section. When this neckline is finished, it looks attractive edged with shells or trimmed with a piece of filet crochet.

Leave another third of the stitches at the center. With the same side facing you as when you began working on the first section, rejoin the yarn to the last third and complete it to match. Unless you are working a totally reversible pattern, don't join the yarn at the outside edge to work the second half or you will notice a distinct change in the appearance of the pattern here. This will also make it easier to pick up stitches later for the edging.

For a curved or round neckline, shape it as decribed in Question 96, slipping across a number of stitches at the center and then decreasing at the neck edge on successive rows for a classic round neck. Pick up stitches for the band or work a separate piece of ribbed crochet and stitch it to the neck to form a funnel or turtleneck.

This neckline can also be divided at the center, working on only half the stitches at a time, in order to insert a zipper or a placket later. You can add a collar by picking up stitches as for a neckband and then increasing on alternate rows to give a gradual curve. Alternatively, you could work a separate piece of crochet in white cotton, which you would stitch to the neckline.

RIGHT Four types of neckline.

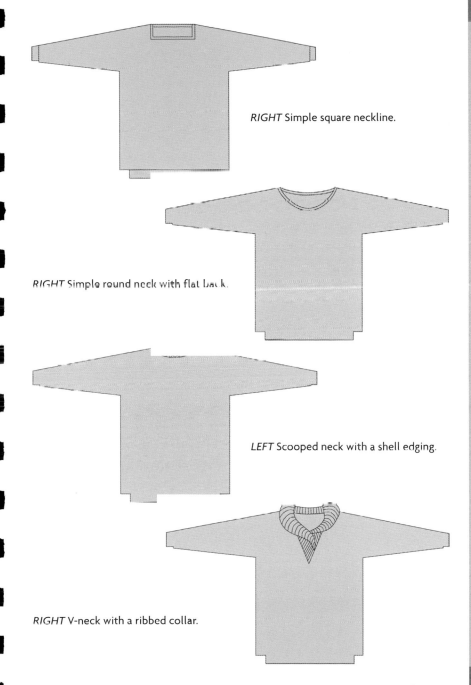

RIGHT Simple square neckline.

RIGHT Simple round neck with flat back.

LEFT Scooped neck with a shell edging.

RIGHT V-neck with a ribbed collar.

Question 101:
What do work straight and reverse shaping mean?

To work straight essentially means to continue in the pattern you are working with as it was set, without the need for any shaping or alteration in stitch count for the required number of rows or length. It is sometimes referred to as "work even" and usually comes just after you have made a series of increases or decreases. Be aware that you may have to start at a different point in the pattern row in order to maintain the design.

Because many crochet stitches are reversible, you may think that you could work the left and right fronts the same. If you examine the stitches closely, you will see that they form a series of ridges and troughs. The work will look neater if these match across the work. In order to do this, you will need to reverse the shaping on each piece.

Reverse shaping means to make a mirror image of a piece you have already worked. Whatever you did at the beginning of one row on the first piece you worked, you then do at the end of the row on the second piece.

For example, if you are working a V-necked cardigan with a set-in sleeve, you will have begun a gradual slope for the "V" at the beginning of the row on the right front and ended by missing a number of stitches for the start of the armhole.

When you start the left front, you begin by slip stitching over a number of stitches for the armhole and end by decreasing in order to form the slope of the V-neck. For the rest of the pattern, you work it just as you did with the first piece. Only the shaping changes.

Question 102:
What other ways of shaping are there?

Another way of making a gradual upward slope is to use stitches of different heights. Changing the number of times you wrap the yarn around the hook before inserting it into the stitch will lengthen the stitch considerably. This method is particularly useful when working irregularly shaped pieces of free-form crochet. It can also be used to make a distinctive pattern of waves, especially where consecutive rows are worked in different colors.

BELOW A piece of free-form crochet showing various ways of shaping.

HOW IT'S DONE

To make a series of waves:

1 Work the first stitch in single crochet, the second in half double crochet, the third in double crochet and so on. For the return, gradually reduce the height of the stitches back to single crochet. Work the next stitch in single crochet before starting the wave again. On the next row, work the longest central stitch over the middle single crochet.

2 Another very simple way of shaping is gradually to change to successively larger hooks. This method is especially useful for shawls or for skirts that are worked from the top down.

7

COLOR WORK

Changes in color create stripes, patches and designs of intricate beauty – working in the colors is a skill that will give you infinite potential to make the patterns you want.

Question 103:
How do I follow a color chart?

Geometric and pictorial designs can be produced in crochet much as they can in knitting, but there is no need for special graph paper. The designs can be worked out on ordinary square graph paper.

When working pictorial designs, it is best to work in single crochet as this is the most square of the stitches. It is also more compact, enabling more detail in the picture. Single crochet also covers the ends of the changes of yarns better than other, more-open stitches. If you are using a longer stitch, then you will need to allow for this on your paper by making two or more rows of squares equal one row of crochet.

To follow the chart, begin with the square at the bottom right (1a).

Then change color and work 1b. Carry both colors along at the back of the work. Continue to work along the row, repeating the chart as many times as necessary. At the end of the row, turn your work and read the second row from left to right, from square 2e, to square 2d, and so on. Remember to carry the colors along on the same side of the work (the wrong side) as you did before.

Alternatively, where there are many changes of color, you can cut off the yarn at the end of the row and keep the same side facing you. Rejoin the new yarns and work again from right to left. Always work from right to left when working in the round, with the same side facing you.

X	X	X	X	X	5
	X	X	X	X	4
		X	X	X	3
			X	X	2
				X	1
e	d	c	b	a	

Question 104:
How do I join in a new color?

The neatest way to change colors is to do it partway through the stitch. Of course, this doesn't work when you are making chains or slip stitches as these involve only one movement. There you simply change the color at the start of the stitch. For single crochet or anything longer, work until you have two loops left on the hook, drop the old yarn, take up the new color, fold it around the hook and draw this loop through the last two left on the hook. The bottom of the stitch is now in the old color, and the top is in the new color. Hold the short end of the new yarn on the wrong side of the work (or the short ends of both yarns if you are not going to need the old color in that position again). Make the next few stitches over the top of them, fastening them in. If you are working an open mesh or a very lacy pattern, it is neater to darn the ends in later rather than work over them.

This method works equally well for crochet worked back and forth or in the round. Where you need to change color at the beginning of a round, before making the required turning chains, fasten off the old yarn and then join in the new one. Work the turning chain(s) with both strands of the new yarn held together. Then work over the short end as above or darn it in at the end.

This latter method is also the one to choose when working wide stripes if you are not going to carry the colors up the side.

LEFT Stages in joining on a new color. Finishing the stitch with the new color (*top*), working the next stitch (*bottom*).

Question 105:
How do I avoid holes when starting a new color?

If you change colors as described in question 104, you will be able to make the change without getting holes between changeovers. There are occasions when you are working on multicolored crochet designs in which you will not be joining in a new color but taking it from an earlier row.

To avoid holes when working in this way, try to remember to catch in a color that will be required in a similar position on a later row. Do this by lifting the contrast color in front of the hook before working the next stitch. On the row where you need to bring it into the work, keep both yarns at the back of the work, take the current color behind the one you need next, work half of the stitch with the current color and then complete it with the new one. If you are working a loose stitch in different colors, it is best to cut off the yarns and rejoin them where necessary as the ends will not be held down properly with long stitches and can easily work free. Darn them in firmly later.

EXPERT TIP

❝If you are working a number of rows before repeating a color, you can keep working over the color you need to repeat later, holding it on the wrong side of alternate rows each time, ready to bring it into the correct place for its next use. Alternatively, you can cut it off and rejoin it each time it is required, fastening in the ends as described on page 121. ❞

Question 106:
How do I carry the yarns across the work?

If your pattern calls for you to work several sections in the same color, such as when you are working checks or patterns similar to those given in the chart on page 120, carry the yarn across the back each time rather than joining on a new piece for each block of color. Simply hold the color that is not being used along the line of stitches, keeping it to the wrong side. Then work the next set of stitches over it.

The work should appear neat on the wrong side, with the carried colors completely hidden. Don't pull tightly on the yarn, but hold it at the same tension as before. If you are using a very bulky yarn, you may not like the extra thickness that this method can produce. In this case, it is better to use separate balls for each section of color.

There are other occasions when you do not carry the yarns across and work over them. That occurs when working raised sections in

contrasting colors. Here you work a number of stitches in the contrasting color and then pull firmly on the main yarn coming from the end of the first section before working the second section with it, forming a pleat.

When you are working several colors along a row, there is no need to carry each of them across the back of the work. Just leave the ends dangling until they are needed on the next row.

RIGHT Carrying a yarn across the work, blending a new color with the first.

Question 107:
How do I stop the yarns from tangling?

This is a perennial question and one that is not always satisfactorily solved. One method is to keep each color in a shoe box, in the correct order, and to turn the box in the same direction as you turn your work at the end of each row. Contrary to the usual advice always to turn your work in the same direction, turn it in opposite directions at the end of each row so that the ends are not constantly twisting around each other.

You may find that balls of yarn roll around the floor. You can either keep each ball in a jar, which has the added advantage of keeping it clean, or place it on a stick similar to that used for holding rolls of paper towel.

Another method of stopping balls of yarn from rolling around is to take the yarn from the middle of the ball. If this is difficult to find, rewind the ball with a wool winder. Taking yarn from the middle of the ball also gives you a more even tension.

A method familiar to knitters is to wind short lengths of yarn onto bobbins. Because of the simplicity in joining on new colors, this method works especially well in crochet.

Color Work

Question 108:
How should I hold the different colors?

When you are working with several colors in a row, as in pictorial crochet, there is no easy way of manipulating all the colors in your hand at once, as there is in Fair Isle knitting, in which you can hold one color in each hand and feed them through as you work your pattern.

The basic method, when it comes to crochet, is simply to drop the old color and then take up the new one. However, you might find that it's slightly quicker, in situations where you have to make several changes in a row, for example, to wrap the yarn around your little finger and just carry it across the palm of your hand. If you use this method, it's important that you take care to keep the same tension in the yarn over the colored section as you do over the rest of the piece.

If you end up with long, loose floats on the back of your piece of crochet where you have not been able to keep an even tension as you work, you can fix this by cutting the strand in the middle and then darning it back into the work, along a few stitches, up or down a row and then back the other way. Thimble-like devices can hold several colors at once on one finger. However, these can take some getting used to and can cause the yarns to tangle.

EXPERT TIP

&& It is possible to hold two colors in your hand at once by keeping one to the front of your finger and one to the back. Carry the one not in use along the back of the work, and crochet over it with the working yarn. Theoretically, it should be possible to carry a third color over a spare finger, but this takes a lot of practice! &&

Question 109:
Can I make stripes with uneven numbers of rows?

Because you are working with only one tool, which has only one loop on it, you don't have to worry about which side has the point and which the end. Therefore, it is easy to work stripes of any numerical value in crochet.

At the end of each stripe of one color, draw up a long loop and pass the whole of the ball through it. It will now be tied into the work. Take up the next color. Starting at whichever end you please, fasten the new yarn to the side with a simple knot, ready to darn in later. Instead, make a slipknot with the new yarn, insert the hook into the first stitch, wrap the yarn over and draw it through the stitch and the slipknot.

Work the next row(s) with the new color. End the contrast color in the same way as above and take up the original color or a new one to work the next row(s). Continue in this way throughout the work. It will be completely reversible, especially if you are working in a stitch that will cover the tail ends successfully.

BELOW Reversible fabric featuring uneven rows of stripes.

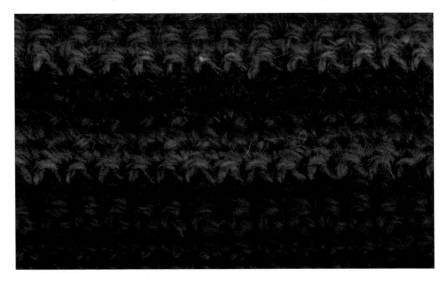

Question 110:
Should I carry the yarns along the sides or break them off?

If you are working narrow stripes, it saves a lot of time darning in if you carry yarn along the sides and take it into the seams later. To avoid any loose loops at the edge of the work, alternate the colors in your turning chain, that is, one chain in A and the second chain in B.

However, if you are working wide stripes or using lots of colors, it may be neater to break off the colors you are not using and either work over them or darn them in later. Darning in is the better method when you are working one of the more-open patterns.

Darn the ends into the last row of a stripe of the same color for the least noticeable effect. Work along the row for a few stitches then up half a stitch and back the other way.

Where the stripes are wide enough, darn the ends in diagonally so they will be less likely to come loose.

ABOVE Strands worked on the wrong side.

LEFT Ball of yarn passed through the loop so that the stitches don't unravel.

Question 111:
How do I make zigzag stripes?

Zigzags and chevrons are formed by making increases and corresponding decreases along the row. They work equally well in a single- or multi-colored stripes. The beginning and end will be shaped. If you want them to look the same, you will need to join two pieces at the center.

To make zigzags, work two stitches into the stitch next to the turning chain, work *x* number of stitches straight, then work three stitches together or two decreases side by side, work *x* number of stitches again then another increase. Repeat this

BELOW A large chevron formed by increasing at each end of the row and decreasing 4 stitches at the center.

group across the row.

Another method is to make one stitch, one chain, one stitch, into the stitch next to the turning chain, then work *x* number of stitches as above and miss two stitches before working *x* number of stitches. This leaves a series of small holes at the increase and decrease points.

Make sure you work the increases and decreases above one another to give a well-defined series of peaks and troughs rather than a series of shallow waves.

Chevrons are also created by using increases and decreases. This time the increases are at each end of the work and the decreases are all at the center.

Question 112:
What is free-form crochet?

Free-form, known as scrumbling, is creative crochet, where randomly shaped and textured pieces are joined when you have finished them all. It is not worked from a pattern but is made up almost as you go along. It is at its most interesting when various yarns of different textures are used and is an ideal way of using up your leftovers. Try out different techniques from all forms of crochet, incorporating lace work, hairpin, Afghan and so on, to produce a variety of shapes.

Each individual shape does not have to be planned. If you are making an item of a particular shape, it is best to make a paper template of the finished shape. Lay the free-form pieces on top of this template as you make them so that you can work out where any extra stitches or shapes need to added and also to see how to shape for neck and armholes if necessary. A symmetrical arrangement seems to work best on pieces that are to be worn. It is easier to plan this if you can see the shape filling up as you go, rather than trying to visualize it.

Question 113:
How do I darn in all my loose ends?

If you are making a piece with no side seams, work a row of single crochet all around the edge after you join the pieces, covering any ends that are left at the outside edges. For the other tail ends, weave them in on the wrong side of the work, across the same color and following the direction of the strands of the stitches. Weave into a stitch across on the next row and then work the ends back in the opposite direction for two or three stitches. Where the stitches are long and loose, work across another stitch and back again in the direction of the first line of weaving.

If you are using a thick yarn that is difficult to thread into a needle, use a crochet hook to pull your ends through each stitch. A size or two smaller than the one you used to work the crochet will be easier to insert into the backs of the stitches.

8

WORKING IN THE ROUND

Creating a circular piece of crochet requires certain methods that differ from other styles of working. Using this style of crochet, however, allows you to create more shapes than simply circles.

Question 114:
How do I start a circular piece of crochet?

Because only one tool is used for crochet, it is very easy to work in the round, either to make flat pieces or tubes. It can be worked as a spiral or in rounds joined with a slip stitch. The work can be turned at the end of each round also making it more reversible. It is usually referred to as circular crochet even though all kinds of shapes can be made this way, including squares.

There are at least three methods to choose from when starting a circular piece of crochet. The first two will leave a small hole at the center of the piece. If you want to avoid this, it's best to follow the third method.

Method 1 Make a short length of foundation chain. Four or five is usually enough. Anything longer than this will make a more definite hole in the center of your finished piece. Once complete, join the last chain to the first with a slip stitch, ready to begin working your next round.

Method 2 Start by making a slipknot, bringing the tail end through the loop rather than the ball end so that you can draw it up a little tighter at the end. You should make three or four chains, depending on the stitch you are going to use: three for a single crochet, four for a double crochet. Your first round of stitches will be worked into the first of these chains, in other words, the third or fourth one from the hook.

Method 3 For the final method, in which no hole will appear in your finished work, begin by wrapping the yarn once or twice around your finger. Carefully remove this circle of yarn from your finger and work your first stitch directly into the hole. Work the rest of the first round of stitches into the hole covering the strands of yarn. If you then pull on the tail end of yarn, it will draw the ring up tightly and close the hole.

Question 115:
How do I work the following rows?

If you have used the first method to make the initial ring, the next step is to make the appropriate number of turning chains above the slip stitch. Next, work the required number of stitches directly into the hole at the center of the ring, remembering that the turning chain is your first stitch. If the pattern calls for 16 stitches in the ring, make the turning chain and then follow with 15 stitches.

Join the last of these stitches to the top of the turning chain with a slip stitch. For the next and subsequent rounds, work into the head of the stitches on the previous round, just as you would for flat crochet.

If you have used the second method for your center ring, the chains that you made to begin with are your turning chain. The rest of the stitches are worked into the chain farthest from the hook, and the work is completed as above.

For the third method, make the required number of turning chains then the rest of the stitches directly

RIGHT Joining the chains with a slip stitch (*top*), working into the first chain (*middle*) and working into a wrapped circle of yarn (*bottom*).

Into the loop of yarn that was wrapped around your finger, covering the tail end of yarn at the same time to secure it firmly in place. You will still be able to draw it up to pull the hole closed.

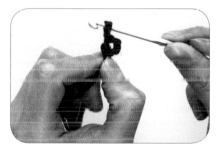

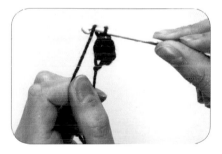

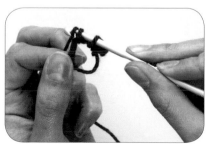

Question 116:
Do I turn the work at the end of each round?

When you reach the end of your first round and you have made the joining slip stitch, you will have to choose whether to continue with the same side facing you or turn the work and continue that way instead.

Whichever way you decide to work, you first need to make a series of chains to bring the hook up to the correct height for the next stitch. You will need two for a half double crochet, three for a double crochet, and so on.

This set of chains will stand as the first stitch, so remember to count it when increasing. If you are working a circular piece that will be used for a table decoration, for instance, it is usual to keep the same side of the work facing you. Most patterns will assume that you do not turn your work. Of course, it's always a good idea to read all the instructions through first to make sure.

Occasionally, to get a different texture in a pattern, you will need to keep the same side of the work always facing you. To do this, you will need to cut off the yarn at the end of each row and rejoin it again at the beginning. You will also always be working into the front loops of the stitch. Stitches worked in this way look different to those worked alternately on the right and wrong sides as in back-and-forth crochet. Look at a piece of circular crochet, and you will see that they look smoother.

EXPERT TIP

66 If you are making other shapes, such as squares or hexagons, if you don't turn your work, you will have to slip stitch across a number of stitches at the beginning of the round in order to be in the right place for the next group of stitches. There is nothing against this method, but I prefer to turn the work at the end of each round. 99

Question 117:
How do I know which is the beginning of the round?

When you are working in the round, the first set of chain stitches that you make are not strictly turning chains, although patterns often refer to them as such. In most cases, you do not turn the work after each round but continue working with the same side facing you. The chains are actually made in order to bring the crochet hook to the required height for the next stitch and to prevent your work from turning into a spiral rather than a series of concentric circles.

The beginning of the round is where you have made the first group of chains. If you look closely, you will see that it has a slightly different appearance than the other stitches. This is not quite so obvious with single crochet. If you get into the habit of counting your stitches on the first few rounds, you will gradually become familiar with the difference and know how to recognize it.

To make it more obvious, you can fasten a piece of colored thread to the top of the first stitch.

BELOW A piece of contrast yarn to mark the first stitch of the round.

Question 118:
How do I fasten neatly at the end?

To fasten your work neatly, when you have worked the last round, join the last stitch to the top of the turning chain with a slip stitch. Break off the yarn, and pull it through the loop on the hook. Weave the loose end of the yarn down through the last stitch, across one stitch and back up through the next one to fasten it firmly.

Alternatively, instead of slip stitching to the last stitch, you can

BELOW A neatly fastened piece of crochet work.

break off the yarn and thread it into a needle. Insert the needle under the top two loops of the first stitch (not the turning chain). Then take it back to the last stitch of your round and insert it from front to back under the back loop of the stitch. Insert it again into the first stitch of the round, and then weave it back down the stitch. Take it across one stitch, and weave up the next one so that it ends on the wrong side. Finish the piece neatly by cutting off any remaining yarn.

Question 119:
How do I keep the circle flat?

When working in the round, you need to make some increases intermittently in order to keep the work flat. If you continue on the same number of stitches, you will end up with a tube rather than the disk you were expecting!

The increases need to be spaced at regular intervals on every round at first. The most reliable method of doing this is to increase in every stitch on the 2nd round, in every alternate stitch on the 3rd round, every 3rd stitch on the 4th round

LEFT Regular increases on each round to keep the circle flat.

and so on until your work is the correct size. Each subsequent round should increase by the number of stitches that were in your first round. However, as you work outward, you may find that you don't need to increase on every round but possibly only on alternate rounds.

This is a matter of trial and error depending on which stitch and perhaps which yarn you are using. The work may look a little uneven when you finish, but it will also flatten out to some extent when it is blocked and pressed.

Question 120:
How do I make a half circle?

Occasionally you may need to make a half circle as a filler for pieces made out of circular motifs. Half circles are sometimes used as edgings on items made up from motifs, such as bedspreads. They are begun in the same way as for a circle, using one of the three methods given on page 132, but they are completed by turning at the end of each row. Once you have worked a number of stitches into the initial ring, turn and make the appropriate number of turning chains before working each row.

In the example here, the half circle is worked in double crochet with a turning chain of three stitches.

BELOW A completed half circle.

Question 121:
How do I make a sun catcher?

Sun catchers, which are pretty craft designs like the glass versions based on Native-American tradition, are made over a metal or plastic ring, such as that used to make lampshades.

The rings themselves first have to be covered, either with single crochet or with added picots, which you can then use to attach the central portion of the sun catcher. To cover the ring with single crochet, make a slipknot on the hook. While holding the ring in your left hand and keeping the yarn at the back of the ring, pass the hook through the ring and catch the yarn. Pull it through, and make one single crochet.

Continue making single crochet stitches all around the ring until it is completely covered. Don't leave any gaps between the stitches. When the ring is full, join the last stitch to the first with a slip stitch, fasten off and weave in the ends.

Next make a circular motif from part of a doily pattern or make up your own, making sure that it's big enough to fit inside the ring when slightly stretched. If you have made picots on your ring cover, you can attach the last round of the center as you go. Otherwise, stitch the center to the ring afterward at as many points as you want.

RIGHT A crocheted sun catcher.

Question 122:
How do I make a shaped piece for a hat?

A hat, when broken down into its constituent parts, is basically just a combination of a flat disk and a large-diameter tube. Therefore, when making one with crochet, you will need to work a mix of increases followed by rounds worked straight. You will need to mark the first stitch of each round as you will be increasing at regular intervals. Make sure that you are not working spirals by mistake. Always join the last stitch of the round to the first stitch with a slip stitch. Then make the correct number of chains to bring the work up to the right height. You can either turn the work or continue with the same side facing you. As usual, be consistent.

The first few rounds are made by gradually increasing as you would for a flat disk, into every stitch on the first round, then every alternate stitch and so on. Keep going until this piece will sit comfortably on the crown of your head. Then work one or two rounds straight and again increase evenly around.

Work a few more rounds straight. Then increase evenly again if necessary, until the hat is the right size for your head.

You can, of course, try the hat on as you go, which is another advantage that crochet has over knitting. If you don't need to make it any bigger, continue working in rounds on the set number of stitches until the hat is long enough. Then fasten the end.

If you want a brim on your hat, work increases again, every stitch or every alternate stitch. Then continue to increase as for a flat disk until the brim is as large as you want it.

You can use the same method to add a brim to a hat that is not made of crochet to give it an extra flair.

Question 123:
How do I make a square?

Though it's known as working in the round, a circle is not the only shape that you can make.

There are a number of different squares that you can make in the round. The most well-known is the granny square, which is a combination of double crochet and chains. The number of chains (if any) that you make between the blocks of doubles is up to you, but the one below has one chain between each block. Begin by making a ring of 5 chains, closed with a slip stitch, then follow the instructions to the right.

BELOW A small granny square.

HOW IT'S DONE

1 3ch, 2dc into the ring, (2ch, 3dc) into the ring 3 times, 2ch and close the circle with a slip stitch.

2 Slip stitch across 3 stitches to bring you to the next chain space, or join in a new color, work (3ch, 2dc, 2ch, 3dc) all into this space, 1ch, then (1ch, 3dc, 2ch, 3dc) into next space 3 more times, 1ch, ss to join. You will see your square beginning to form with 2 blocks worked in each corner space.

3 Same as row 2 but work a block of 3dc into the 1ch spaces as well.

4 Continue in this way, adding more rounds with 2 blocks in each corner and 1 block in each chain space.

Question 124:
How do I make a rectangle?

Strictly speaking, a rectangle is not a circular piece of crochet because it is started off on a foundation chain in the same way as a straight piece of crochet. However, once you have worked around both sides of the initial chain, you continue in the round with extra stitches at the corners as for a square. It is a useful way of beginning a rectangular afghan for a bedspread or throw.

A rectangular motif is made in the same way as a square one, again by working in the round rather than the basic crochet manner. In this case, you begin the process on a length of foundation chain rather than a circle and then make extra stitches between the corners. To make a rectangle, follow the directions in the box below.

HOW IT'S DONE

To make a rectangle:

1 Make 16 chain.

2 In the 4th chain from the hook, work 2dc, 2ch, 3dc, 2ch, 3dc.

3 Miss 2ch and work 3dc into the next one, along the row until you reach the end.

4 In the last stitch (the one that was the first of your foundation chains), work 3dc, 2ch, 3dc, 2ch, 3dc.

5 That completes 2 corners and one side.

6 Next work along the other side of the foundation chain, working groups of 3dc into the same stitches as you made the groups on the first side.

7 When you reach the corner, join to the top of the turning chain with a slip st, turn and work 3ch, 2dc into the first space, and so on along the row until you have worked into every space.

8 Work 2 sets of groups into each of the spaces at the corners, and then work back along the other side.

9 Continue like this, working 2 groups into each corner space on every round.

Question 125:
How do I make a triangle?

Again, there are a few variations on crochet triangles, some of which are more open than others. They are all started the same way: on a ring of single or double crochet. Begin with 12sc into a ring, and then join them with a slip stitch. To complete the triangle, follow the instructions in the box to the right.

LEFT A crochet triangle, worked in the round.

Question 126:
How do I make a pentagon?

It is possible to make all kinds of motifs in circular crochet simply by increasing at different points around the circle. To make a granny pentagon, follow the instructions to the right.

HOW IT'S DONE

1 Make your initial circle with 4 chains then work 5 groups of 3dc, each separated by 3ch.

2 On the next round, work (2dc, 2ch, 2dc) into each of the chain spaces.

3 On the following rounds, work (2dc, 2ch, 2dc) into each corner but work 3dc into each of the spaces along the sides.

For a more attractive pentagon with a spiral motif:

1 Make a ring of 5ch and work (6ch, 1dc) 5 times into the ring.

2 (6ch, 3dc in arch) 5 times.

3 (6ch, 3dc in next arch, 1dc in each of next 2dc) 5 times.

4 (6ch, 3dc in next arch, 1dc in each of next 4dc) 5 times.

5 Work 3 more rounds as round 3 until there are 13dc between arches.

6 *5ch, 1dc in center of next arch, 5ch, miss 1dc, 1dc in each dc but last one; rep from * 4 more times.

7 *(5ch, 1dc in next arch) twice, 5ch, miss 1dc, 1dc in each of next dc but last one; rep from * 4 more times.

8 Continue working as 8th round but working an extra 5ch arch in each side and reducing the number of dcs in the blocks until there are 3.

9 (Last round) 5ch, 1dc in next arch, *(3ch, 1dc in next arch) 5 times, 3ch, 1tr in 2nd dc, 3ch, 1dc in arch; rep from * 4 more times, ending with ss to 1st dc.

Question 127:
How do I make a hexagon?

You can probably work out from what you've learned in the previous questions how to make a basic granny hexagon by now. However, if you'd like to try something a little more ornate, you could make one that forms an attractive flower shape by using clusters at the center.

HOW IT'S DONE

Make a ring, work 1ch, 12sc into ring.

1 1ch, 1sc in same st (7ch, miss 1sc, 1sc in next sc) 5 times, 3ch, miss 1sc, 1tr in top of 1st sc.

2 3ch 4dc in 1st arch (3ch, 5dc in next arch) 5 times, 3ch, sl st to top of 3ch.

3 3ch, 1dc in each of next 4c, 3ch, 1sc in next arch, 3ch*, 1dc in each of next 5 stitches, rep from * 4 times then from * to ** again, sl st to top of 3ch.

4 3ch, work 4dctog, *(5ch, 1sc in next arch) twice, 5ch**, 5dctog, rep from *4 times, then from * to **, sl st to 1st cluster.

5 sl st into each of next 3ch, 1ch, 1sc in same st, *5ch, 1sc in next arch, 3ch (5dc, 3ch, 5dc) in next arch, 3ch, 1sc in next arch; rep from * 5 times, ending sl st to 1st sc.

Question 128:
How do I make flowers?

The best-known flower made with crochet is the Irish crochet rose. Instructions for it are in Chapter 9. Flower shapes made from groups of double crochet can be used as decoration. Similar shapes can be joined to form afghans or shawls.

Because flower shapes are not geometrical, they can be hard to join. Shapes not butting together well can be filled with small motifs like stars. The last round of a flower can be made of shells to give a scalloped edge, as in the flower described here.

HOW IT'S DONE

Make a ring and work 3ch, 15dc into it.

1 Join with a sl st 5ch, 1dc in same st, *1ch, miss 1st, (1dc, 2ch, 1dc) in next st; rep from *, ending 1ch, sl st into 3rd ch.

2 sl st into 1st space, 3ch (1dc, 2ch, 2dc) in same place, *1ch (2dc, 2ch, 2dc) in next space; rep from *, ending 1ch, sl st to 3rd ch.

3 sl st to next 2ch space, 3ch, 6dc in same space, 1sc in next ch sp (7dc in next space, 1sc in next space) 7 times, sl st to 3rd ch.

All of the motifs can be worked in more than one color. They look much more interesting worked with a different color for each round.

Question 129:
How do I join the shapes?

The shapes or motifs that you make can either be made individually and then joined together later or can often be joined as you work. The advantage of joining them later is that they are small projects that can easily be carried with you. You can also move them around before joining them to find the best way to place them.

To join them together after they are all finished, stitch them with matching or contrasting yarn by oversewing through the back loops. You can instead crochet them together with single crochet, placing the right sides together and inserting the hook under the strands of both thicknesses together. For a more open seam that looks especially attractive on shawls, work three or four chains and then work a single crochet into one of the motifs, work three or four more chains and work a single crochet further along on the second motif.

To join the motifs together as you work, finish the first shape and then work as far as the last round on the second one. Place the first shape behind it with right sides together and partially work a stitch before completing it through both motifs at the same time. Motifs with a last round of chains or picots are especially easy to join in this way.

Some shapes will not fit together easily and will leave large spaces between them. These can be filled with a few chain stitches or with another smaller motif.

BELOW Several shapes joined together.

9
CROCHET LACE

Delicate pieces of intricate lace can be made using almost the same crochet methods as those used with chunkier yarns, such as wool.

Question 130:
What is crochet lace?

There are various forms of crochet lace, but most are characterized by the use of fine thread, often silk or cotton, and a small hook. The best-known forms of crochet lace are filet crochet and Irish crochet.

Both of these types of crochet developed as a less-expensive form of needle or bobbin lace, which they attempted to imitate. However, they soon became crafts in their own right. Irish crochet can be more fine and intricate than many needle-made laces.

BELOW A piece of crochet lace.

There are also various lacy stitches, often referred to as open crochet lace. These are formed by working a number of chains on every row. The easiest of these is chain lace, which is worked as described.

HOW IT'S DONE

1 Make a foundation chain that is a multiple of 4 plus 6 stitches.

2 Work a sc into 6th ch, *5ch, miss 3ch, 1sc in next ch; rep from * to end, turn.

3 Pattern row: *5ch, 1sc in next arch; rep from * to end. Repeat this row for the lace.

Question 131:
What is filet crochet?

Filet is another form of crochet that was derived from lace. It is distinguished from other types of lace by its designs, which are based on squares. While an open mesh forms the basis of the design, some squares are filled in and referred to as blocks. The open squares are known as spaces. There are also slightly more-elaborate stitches known as bars and lacets. Reversed lacets form diamond shapes. The meshes can be of different sizes. The blocks that form the designs are worked in the stitch appropriate to the size of the mesh.

Some of the older patterns gave instructions for filet crochet row by row. If you are working from one of these, it is easier to follow if you turn it into a chart. Working from charts has the added advantage that you can use any size of mesh and also follow a chart from any

RIGHT A piece of filet crochet, distinguishable by its square pattern.

country in the world.

Once you have learned to work from a chart and understand the way that the designs are represented, it is a simple matter to create designs of your own.

Question 132:
What is the best yarn for filet crochet?

Filet crochet was traditionally worked in white or cream cotton using a small hook. This was because it was intended to be used where a more-expensive lace would be employed, such as on household linens, collars, petticoats or handkerchiefs. Fine silk was often used for higher-quality items.

However, there is no reason why any type of yarn that has a smooth finish cannot be used. It needs to be smooth to allow the openness of the mesh and the outline of the design to be clearly seen. You don't want to be filling the spaces with hairy or eyelash yarns, or you will lose the crispness of the design.

Many people hold the opinion that filet crochet looks its best when worked with a fine hook and thread, preferably cotton, which launders well and retains some firmness to show off the designs to best advantage. Cotton can also be stiffened easily if necessary, using starch or sugar solution to create three-dimensional pieces.

The most-detailed designs are obtained when using very fine thread, such as Coats or DMC 100. This will give a gauge of approximately ten squares to 1 inch (2.5 cm); 20 cotton will give a gauge of approximately five squares to 1 inch (2.5 cm).

LEFT A ball of crochet cotton suitable for filet or Irish crochet.

Question 133:
How do I start a piece of filet crochet?

Most pieces of filet are symmetrical and worked back and forth in rows. It is possible to make all kinds of shapes. Circular pieces can be made by beginning with a short length of chain and increasing blocks and spaces at each end of the rows until it is the required diameter. You then work a few rows straight before decreasing blocks and spaces back to the number in the first row.

The number of chains you make at the beginning depends on the size of mesh. Because the foundation row can end up tighter than the rest of the work, it is often worthwhile to use a one size larger hook for this row. This will also make it easier to find the stitches for the next row. Some people find it easier to work a row of single crochet into the foundation row rather than beginning the pattern right away. Remember to end with a row of single crochet to keep it symmetrical. Do not begin with one of the alternative foundation rows as this would spoil the geometry.

Question 134:
How do I know how many chains to make in my foundation row?

If you are following a pattern with written instructions as well as a chart, this should tell you how many chains to make at the beginning. If you are following a chart alone, or one of your own designs, you will need to work out how many chains to begin with. The spaces are allocated the same number of chains as the blocks. For a medium, or standard, mesh, which is the one most frequently used, you need three chains for each block or space on the chart plus three chains for the turning chain. For a small mesh, make two chains for each block or space and three chains for the turning chain. For a large mesh, make three chains for each block or space and four chains for the turning chain.

For example, to make a mesh of eight squares in medium mesh, make a chain 8 x 3 = 24 plus 3 for the turning chain.

Question 135:
How do I make the mesh for filet crochet?

There are three different sizes of mesh for filet crochet, as stated on the previous page: small, medium and large. Medium, or standard, mesh is the one most often used. It is made by working one double crochet and two chains for every square. To make a standard mesh, begin by making your foundation row and turning chain and then follow the instructons in the box below. These terms are used for whichever thickness of yarn and size hook are used. It is the method of working that determines the name applied to the mesh.

HOW IT'S DONE

1 If your first row consists of all spaces, make 2 chains, miss 2 chains and work 1 double crochet into the next chain.

2 Repeat this sequence to the end of the row. Turn, make 3 chain to stand as the first double crochet, *make 2 chains and work 1 double crochet into the top of the double crochet on the previous row.

3 Repeat from * to the end of the row and continue working like this for every space.

4 If you need to work a block instead of a space, work 2 double crochet into the space of the previous row.

5 There will also be 1 double crochet on each side of these two stitches, which makes each block look as though it contains 4 stitches. However, one of the double crochets actually belongs to the previous square or block, so in fact, each block is made up of 3 double crochet.

Small mesh is made by working in double crochet with one chain between each, so there is only one double crochet in a space to make a block. Large mesh is made with two chains again, but this time working triples between them instead of double crochet.

Question 136:
How do I read a filet crochet chart?

Charts are drawn as though the work is lying flat and the front of the work is facing you. The lower line on the chart is the first row of spaces and/or blocks. The squares are often numbered along the bottom for each square and up the side for the rows. One square on the chart represents one block or space. The open squares represent spaces, and the filled in ones are the blocks. There are also some squares with different symbols in them to represent bars, lacets and diamonds.

After you have made your foundation chain, make the turning chain to stand as the first stitch. Then read the chart along the bottom from the square on the right. In the case of the chart below, the first row will be made entirely of 13 spaces.

Read the chart from right to left, completing the squares according to whether they are empty or filled. Turn your work at the end of the row, and read the chart from left to right along the second row of squares. Continue in this way, working up from the bottom to the top of the chart and reading odd rows from right to left and even rows from left to right.

1	2	3	4	5	6	7	8	9	10	11	12	13	
													9
			X						X				8
		X		X				X	X	X			7
	X		X		X		X	X	X	X	X		6
X		X	X	X		X	X	X	X			X	5
	X	X	X	X	X		X		X		X		4
		X	X	X			X		X				3
			X					X					2
													1

☐ = space   X = block (or filled square)

Question 137:
How do I measure the gauge?

Before you begin a piece of filet crochet, it is a good idea to work a test piece in different meshes and with your chosen yarn. Some people find that the large mesh will give a more square shape to the blocks and spaces than the medium, or standard. However, it is up to you to decide whether this matters.

Make a test piece at least 5 inches (12 cm) square, using a mixture of blocks and spaces. Then block and press it as you would for your finished piece. Let it dry. Then lay it on a flat surface. With a rigid ruler, measure 4 inches (10 cm) across one row of squares.

Count how many squares you have to 1 inch (2.5 cm). Do the same with the rows. If you have fewer squares than recommended, try a smaller hook. If you have too many squares, use a larger one.

Sometimes the spaces will work out smaller than the blocks. Unless there is a huge discrepancy, this should even itself out in the finishing process. Unless you are working precise measurements to fit around a tablecloth or to make something to wear, for example, it is not usually as important in filet to achieve exactly the correct measurements. However, you do need to choose a gauge that will give you a good contrast between the blocks and spaces in order to see the motifs clearly.

BELOW To measure the stitch and row gauge, count each filled and empty square. There are 30 rows to 4 inches in this example.

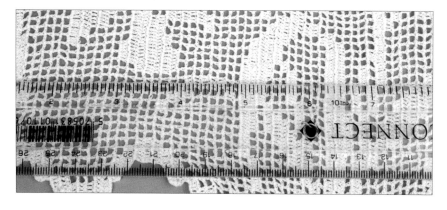

Question 138:
Are there any other stitches used in filet crochet?

Most filet pieces you will encounter use just the basic mesh. There are some more-intricate stitches that can be used to embellish the work.

The most popular of these is a raised stitch worked in place of a block. It is worked in the same way as a cluster in ordinary crochet. In other words, extra double crochet stitches are worked into the block. However, the last loop of each stitch is left on the hook and then the thread is drawn through all of the loops and finished with a slip stitch.

Alternatively, each of the first few double crochets are completed and then the last loop of the last one is drawn through and fastened with a slip stitch.

You can also make larger spaces linked with several chains:

The single crochet is worked into the center of the 9ch on the 2nd row and into the chain of the previous row on the 3rd row.

The only other technique you may come across is when working corners. Here you complete one section of an edging, rejoin the thread to the inner corner and work into the sides of the stitches of the first section, as you would when picking up stitches for a band or neckline. If the corners are mitered, that is, worked on the diagonal, you may need to keep turning the work for alternate rows. There will usually be arrows on the chart to indicate in which direction you should be working.

There are also stitches worked over two rows which are known as lacets and bars.

X	X	X	9ch	X	)(	X
X		X	4ch, 1sc, 4ch	X		X
X		X	4ch, 1sc, 4ch	X		X
X	X	X	9ch	X	X	X

Question 139:
How do I make lacets and bars?

Bars are easier to make and are simply a number of chains spanning two squares. Work a double crochet into the double crochet of the row before, make five chains (four if you are working small mesh), miss the next double crochet and work a double crochet into the following one.

Lacets are worked on the next row, directly above the bar, by working two chains and then a single crochet into the five-chain space, two more chains, and then a double crochet into the next double crochet.

If you are working a lacet above two blocks and spaces, work the single crochet into the double crochet at the center of the two. More than one lacet or bar can be worked alongside each other as well as above each other.

Lacets can also be worked upside down, forming diamond shapes. They are made by working two chains, then two double crochet decreased together, before working two more chains.

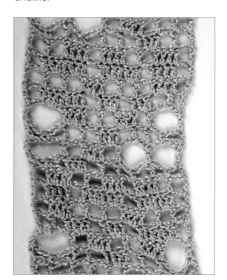

RIGHT Filet crochet with lacets and bars.

Question 140:
How do I work a block into a bar or lacet?

Bars and lacets spread over two squares. To work first a space and then a block, work one double crochet into the first double crochet, make two chains and then work three double crochet directly into the space, not into the strands of any of the chains. Work a double crochet into the next double crochet and continue as per the chart. If you need a block and then a space, work one double crochet into the first double crochet, then three more double crochet into the space followed by two chains and a double crochet into the next double crochet.

To make a block and then a space over a lacet, work one double crochet into the double crochet, work two double crochet into the curved space and one double crochet into the single crochet at the center. Make two chains and complete as per the chart.

When working into a reverse lacet or diamond, work the central double crochet into the diamond space and not into the head of the stitches.

Question 141:
How do I increase a space at the beginning of a row?

To increase a space at the start of a row, work extra chains at the end of the previous row. To increase one space of medium mesh at the end of the row, work two chains for the base of the space then three turning chains as the first double crochet.

Work two more chains for the top of the space, turn, make a double crochet into the top of the next stitch, and continue in pattern.

To increase more than one space,

work as many chains as you need, 3 for each space, then make the turning chain. Work 2ch, 1dc into 3rd chain all along the extra stitches.

This method is used for small and large mesh. For small mesh work, make one chain for the base of the square, two turning chains, and one chain for the top of the square. For large mesh, work two chains, four turning chains and two more chains for the top of the space.

Question 142:
How do I increase a space at the end of a row?

There is a slightly different technique involved when you wish to have the increased space at the end of the same row as one you already increased at the beginning. Because the hook is at the wrong height to work extra chain stitches, you have to perform a slightly more complicated action.

Work two chains, then wrap the yarn four times around the hook. This will make an extra-long stitch to give the length required for the two chains at the base as well as the double crochet.

Insert the hook into the base of the last double crochet of the row, actually into the stitch itself, wrap the yarn around the hook again and draw it through the stitch; *yarn around hook again and draw through two loops.

Repeat this last movement from * twice more until there is one loop left on the hook. The resulting stitch is long enough to act as the base of the square plus one double crochet.

It is known as a triple. To increase more than one space at the end of the row, work as above. This time insert the hook halfway down the side of the triple after working the first two chains.

If you are working small mesh, wrap the yarn around the hook three times to make a triple. For long mesh, wrap the yarn around five times to work a quadruple triple.

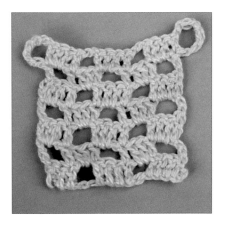

ABOVE Spaces increased at the beginning and end of the row.

Question 143:
How do I increase a block at the beginning of a row?

The method for increasing a block is the same as for increasing a space, but this time you work extra double crochet stitches instead of chains. For medium mesh, make two chains at the end of the row before you want the extra block. Then make three turning chains for the first double crochet. Turn your work, and make the next double crochet into the second of the two newly made chains, that is the fourth chain from the hook, followed by another double crochet into the first of the two chains, which was the fifth chain from the hook. Work one double crochet into the last double crochet of the previous row, and then continue in pattern across the row.

To increase more than one block in medium mesh, add two chains for the first block, and three more chains for each additional block plus three turning chains to stand as the first stitch. Work one double crochet in the fourth chain from the hook and one into each chain.

In most cases, these instructions will be given in the pattern. Earlier patterns assumed a greater level of experience than we do now. Instructions would often simply state "add one mesh" meaning a block or a space. The worker would be left to decide which was most appropriate according to the pattern.

EXPERT TIP

66 For small mesh, make four chains, then work one double crochet into the 4th chain from the hook; for large mesh make six chains and work one triple in the 5th chain from the hook. 99

Question 144:
How do I increase a block at the end of a row?

To increase one block at the end of the row, you make extra-long stitches as for increasing a space. This time, you wrap the yarn twice around the hook and then insert it into the base of the last stitch. This has made the first double crochet of the new block plus a portion of the stitch to extend its width, which actually makes it a triple. You now need to make two more triples, wrapping the yarn twice around the hook but then inserting

the hook into the base of the stitch that you just made. Complete the stitch as before. Then repeat the procedure again for the last stitch of the block.

If you need to add more than one block, continue adding more triples, working into the base of the preceding one each time until you have a multiple of three new stitches. Again, adjust the number of wraps and/or stitches according to the size mesh you are making.

All of these increasing methods leave a series of short steps along the side. This is a feature of the designs when working decorative edgings or household linen. You may want a more gradual slope for a neck or an armhole edge of a garment. In this case, simply work an extra double crochet into the first and last stitches.

For an increased space, work two chains and then a double crochet into the last stitch. To decrease a block or space, miss the two chains of the last space and work a double crochet into the last stitch.

LEFT A piece of crochet with an increased end block.

Question 145:
How do I make stepped edges?

To make a series of steps at the side edges of a piece of filet, increase one or two squares at the edge of each row or each alternate row, as given in the instructions for increasing on pages 159-162. When you have enough stitches at the central point of your step, either decrease gradually back to the original number again or decrease several squares at once on the same row to give sharper points.

To make a decorative edge at the lower edge of a piece, you will need to work little sections separately and then join them together. To join two sections together, finish section one and leave it attached to the ball. Start a new ball and work section two; stop before you reach the last row.

Partially work the turning chain of section two. Then break off the yarn and complete this section with the yarn from section one. For a shaped edge at the top of the work, complete each small section and fasten off the thread before rejoining it to complete the second section, and so on.

BELOW Stepped edges on a piece of filet crochet.

Question 146:
How do I increase a lacet or a bar?

It is very unlikely that the extreme edge of crochet would be comprised of lacets and bars. If you should come across a pattern where they are present, bars are increased in the same way as spaces but making three extra chains for the five-chain space.

To increase a lacet at the beginning of a row, make five chains for the base, three for the double crochet then three more chains, a single crochet into the central chain of the first five chains, three chains for the second half of the lacet and one double crochet into the next double crochet.

To increase a bar at the end of a row, make five chains for the top of the bar. Wrap the yarn seven times around the hook and complete the stitch as for a new space, drawing the hook through two loops at a time.

To increase a lacet at the end of a row, work three chains, wrap the yarn twice around the hook and work one double triple into the last stitch of the row, make 3 more chains then a triple triple into the point where the two groups of three chains meet. Your hook should now be at the top, ready to turn and work the next row.

To decrease one space in a lacet or bar, work only halfway across it before turning.

Question 147:
Can I work filet crochet in the round?

Filet crochet is normally worked flat, back and forth, but it is possible to work it in the round. The method is similar to that of making squares in the round. Begin with a small circle, formed by whichever method you choose, and then increase stitches at the corners. There will be a diagonal line of holes from the center to each corner. For this reason, it is not the best method for working pictorial designs. These are best worked using the increasing and decreasing method.

To begin a piece of filet worked in the round, make a starting chain or a circle of yarn. Then work as follows: 3 chain, 3 double crochet into circle, 3 chain, 4 double crochet into circle, 3 chain, 4 double crochet into circle, 3 chain, 4 double crochet into circle, 3 chain and join with a slip stitch to the top of the first set of 3 chain. This completes your first round with each of the 3-chain spaces forming the corners. Work blocks or spaces as required in the 3-chain spaces with 3 more chains between them on each round.

Question 148:
What is Irish crochet?

Like filet crochet, Irish crochet was devised as a means of copying a more-expensive needle lace, in this case guipure lace with its raised motifs on a net background. It is thought that it was first worked by nuns, who then taught it to women in Ireland at the time of the potato famine. It is often referred to as "Nun's Work" or "Poor Man's Lace."

Its chief characteristic is a design of raised motifs, usually leaves and flowers, combined with an open mesh background. The background is made by working a number of chain stitches which are joined to the motifs after they have been worked. Sometimes the background is a ready-made machine-made net with the motifs stitched onto it. The best forms are those made entirely in crochet and with a background mesh that also has some decorative stitches, such as picots or knots.

Question 149:
What yarn and stitches do I use?

The traditional yarn used for Irish crochet is 70 or 100 white or cream cotton worked with a fine steel hook size 12 (1.00 mm) or smaller. This gives the closest imitation of needle-made lace. However, imitation of another craft is no longer the purpose of Irish crochet, because it is now seen as a skilled craft in its own right.

As with filet crochet, any smooth yarn can be used to make a modern piece of Irish crochet. However, the very finely worked pieces with many motifs and meshes made from 100 cotton cannot be surpassed for their beauty and delicacy.

The stitches used are the basic ones found in ordinary crochet. Sometimes they are worked through only the back loop to give a raised effect, and some stitches are worked over padding threads to give an even more three-dimensional effect. Picots and bullion knots are frequently incorporated. There is also a stitch unique to Irish crochet known as a clones knot, which you will read about on page 171.

BELOW Samples of fine cotton yarn.

Question 150:
How do I make the motifs?

There are various traditional shapes in Irish crochet, but there is also no reason why you cannot invent some of your own. The most well-known motifs are leaves and roses. You may also find patterns for shamrocks, triangles and curlicues, among others.

Because the motifs are made separately, there is no reason why they cannot be worked in a different color than the background. There are some very beautiful pieces made from groups of leaves and flowers in contrasting colors.

BELOW An Irish crochet leaf motif.

Question 151:
How do I make some of the other motifs?

HOW IT'S DONE

To make a shamrock:

1 Make 17 chains , work a slip stitch into the 10th chain from the hook to form a circle, leaving 7 chains for the stem.

2 First leaf: work (3sc, 3dc, 5tr, 3dc, 3sc) all into the circle

3 Second leaf: * make 10 chains, sl st into the same 10th chain as the slip stitch of the first leaf. Keeping the same side of the work facing you, turn the work through 90° and work (3sc, 3dc, 5tr, 3dc, 3sc) all in the second circle.

4 Repeat from * for the third leaf.

5 Sl st into the same 10th chain then work along the stem with 1sc in ea chain.

6 Fasten off and darn in ends.

HOW IT'S DONE

The other traditional favorite motif is the Irish Rose:

1 Make 8ch and join with a slip stitch to form a ring.

2 1st round: 1ch, 16sc into ring, sl st into 1st sc.

3 2nd round: 1ch, sc into 1st sc, *5ch, miss 1 sc, 1sc into next sc*, rep from * to * 6 more times, 5ch, sl st into 1st sc.

4 3rd round: sl st into 1st arch, 1ch, then in each arch work *1sc, 5hdc, 1sc* sl st into 1st sc (8 petals)

5 4th round: 1ch, working behind each petal, make 1sc into the 1st stitch of the 2nd round, *6ch, 1sc into next sc on round 2*, rep from * to * 6 more times, ch 6, sl st into 1st sc.

6 5th round: sl st into 1st arch, 1ch, *1sc, 6hdc, 1sc* into each arch, sl st into 1st sc

For more layers of petals, work further rounds, increasing the number of chains in each arch and the number of half double crochet worked into them.

Question 152:
What are padding threads?

In order to make the motifs stand out from the crochet background they are sitting on, many motifs are worked in relief. To achieve this, the crochet is worked over other threads, known as padding threads. These can be a number of strands of the same yarn as used for the main work or a thicker yarn or cord, depending on how raised you want the motifs to be. The padding threads are not used to make stitches but are laid across the work. Then a series of single crochet stitches are made over them.

To make the work stand out from the background even more, a row of double crochet stitches are sometimes worked over the top of this row of single crochet.

Question 153:
How do I make the background mesh?

There are several different meshes, depending on how ornate you want the piece to be. Begin by tacking the motifs into position on a paper or cloth template. Then work a length of crochet for a border. Next, take a slightly thinner thread than that used for your main work.

The simplest mesh is made by working a number of chain stitches, five or six, and then working a single crochet into the border. Work another set of chains and another single crochet further along the border. Continue in this way until you reach the end of the border. Then turn and work back with five chains and a single crochet into the first five-chain arch. Complete this row. On the next row, still work the five-chain arches as before. When you get to a motif, work two chains and a single crochet into the edge of the motif, two more chains and single crochet into the arch.

Continue like this, filling in the spaces between the motifs with arches. Finish off with a row of shells or make another border and link this to the arches as before.

A more-decorative mesh is made by working one or more picots along the chains at intervals. Of course, you can also use double or triple crochet stitches instead of singles and chains.

Question 154:
What is a clones knot?

The clones knot is another piece of raised work often included in Irish crochet. It looks like a small ball. It is formed by working five or six chain stitches, then wrapping the thread around the hook several times, as for the bullion stitch, and working over the top of these chains.

Cross the hook to the left of the chains and catch the thread, cross the hook to the right and catch another thread. Continue these two movements until you have about ten loops on the hook. Wrap the thread around the hook again, and draw it through all ten of them. Wrap the thread around the hook

again, and draw it through the loop to fasten it off. Make your next stitch into the first stitch of the series of chains to form a small ball.

Sometimes your hook will be difficult to draw through all of the loops. If this happens, push it from right to left into the loops until they are stretched a bit more, and then try drawing it back again.

Clones knots can be used as accents along a series of chains or around the edges of motifs.

BELOW Clones knots.

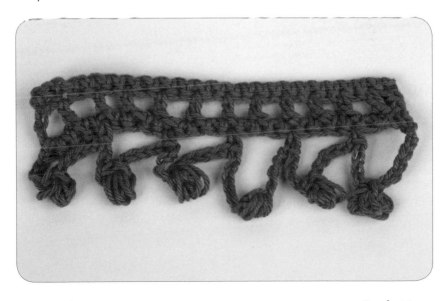

10
FOLLOWING PATTERN INSTRUCTIONS

Most garments and other items in crochet are made from a pattern. Understanding them – and learning to alter and create them – is a vital skill to learn.

Question 155:
How do I read a crochet pattern?

Pattern instructions these days are standardized, making the instructions much easier to follow. Nowadays, as well as standard abbreviations, there are also International Crochet Symbols (see Useful Information). This means that you can follow a crochet pattern written in any language where the instructions are given in chart form. It's not just the working instructions that you need to follow – there are also notes on size, materials, gauge, and possibly, level of experience.

The information on materials will tell you how many balls of yarn you need. This could be different for each size, so make sure that you relate your size to the correct amount. When the pattern calls for several different colors, the instructions will also contain a symbol or code name for each of these; for example, MC for main color; A for first contrast color; B for second contrast; and so on.

In clothing, as you can see from the chart, the actual measurement of a piece is not always the same as the bust or chest size. You may prefer a garment to be tighter or looser than the one that fits your size, so check the measurements given in the instructions before deciding which size to make. Note how many balls of yarn are required for this size, too. Read through the pattern carefully, and note whether the work is to be made in rows or rounds. If it is in rounds, see if you turn the work at the end of each round or continue with the same side facing you.

Sizes	S	M	L
Bust size	32	36	40
Actual measurement	36	40	44
Length	24	25	26
Sleeve	17	17	17

Materials: 10 (10, 11) 50g sportweight. 110 yards; Hook size I/9

Question 156:
What does "crochet a chain in multiples of 6 plus 2" mean?

These kind of instructions will be given in a printed pattern when you need to know exactly how many chains to start with for the base row. In this case, you would need to make perhaps 74 chains, which would give you 12 groups of 6 stitches plus 2 at the beginning for your turning chain.

Similar instructions are given for stitch patterns. If you are trying a stitch or substituting a different one, you will want to know how many chains to work to be able to fit complete groups into a row and also to be able to place the groups to best advantage across the row. For example, if the groups are made up of a large number of stitches, you might want to centralize one of them and perhaps work only half groups at each end of the row. You will need to know how many chains you need for each group of stitches that make up the stitch pattern, such as a shell or cluster, and whether this particular stitch will then suit the size you are making. If a pattern repeats over a large number of stitches, you may not be able to use it for your size at that gauge.

Question 157:
What do "yo" and "yoh" mean?

Both of these mean the same thing: take the yarn over the hook. The term is misleading as you don't usually need to maneuver the yarn over the hook. Simply catch it from behind the stitch and hold it in the throat of the hook. Old patterns may refer to the movement as "take up thread, or yarn," which more accurately describes the way that you do it. They may simply tell you to "draw the hook through." It means that you have some yarn on the hook as you couldn't draw it through unless you had!

You may see terms such as "yo4," which means take the yarn over the hook four times to make an extra long, or quadruple, triple. Yarn overs are also sometimes referred to as wraps, especially when making such stitches as the bullion stitch.

Question 158:
How do I follow a chart?

Charts for color work and filet crochet have been explained in the appropriate chapters. There are also charts for crochet worked in the round. These may look complex at first, especially where only one segment is printed. Once you get used to working from them, they are easier to follow than long printed instructions. The chart below is a representation of part of a doily pattern to be worked in the round. It begins with 7 chains to form a ring. Then each round is numbered along the edge. See the table opposite for what the pattern means.

○ = chain
| = single crochet
+ = double crochet
⅄ = cluster

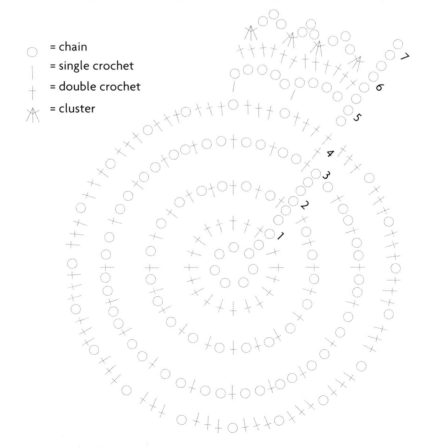

HOW IT'S DONE

Begin with 7 chains joined in a circle.

Round 1: 3ch, 19dc into ring, join with a slip stitch.

Round 2: 3ch, (1dc, 1ch) into each dc, join with slip stitch.

Round 3: 3ch (1dc, 2ch) into each dc, join with slip stitch.

Round 4: 3ch, 3dc in first space (1ch, 3dc) into each space to end, 1ch, join with slip stitch.

Round 5: 6ch (1sc, 5ch) into each space, join with slip stitch.

Round 6: 3ch, (6dc in each loop) to end, join with slip stitch.

Round 7: 3ch, 1 cluster over next 2dc, (3ch, 1 cluster over next 3dc); to end, join with slip stitch.

Question 159:
What does * mean in the instructions?

An asterisk (*) is used to mark the beginning of a section of pattern that you will repeat either across the whole row or round or for a number of times. Read the instructions following the asterisk, and repeat all of that section. If the stitches after the asterisk are to be repeated a number of times and not right to the end of the row, there will often be an asterisk at the beginning and at the end of the section to be repeated. Many older patterns would place two asterisks side by side (**) to denote end of section to be repeated. Repeat only the portion from * to **, and then work any stitches beyond the asterisks.

EXPERT TIP

66 There are also patterns where asterisks are used in place of parentheses and brackets. In this case, there might be a group of stitches between single asterisks, to be repeated *x* times, and then another group of stitches between pairs of asterisks to be repeated however many times. Don't repeat the whole group. Work only those stitches between the same pairs of asterisks the number of times you are instructed in each case. 99

Question 160:
Why are some numbers in parentheses ()?

A pattern will most likely be written for more than one size, so there needs to be a way of differentiating between these. Parentheses are used to distinguish the different sizes. The smallest will usually be given first, outside the parentheses, with the other sizes inside the parentheses in ascending order. Where other numbers occur in the pattern in the same format, these are the number of stitches or rows that you need to work for each size. They will be in the same order outside and inside the parentheses as the sizes.

It is a good idea to highlight your particular size all the way through the pattern, especially where a large range of sizes is given.

Parentheses can also be used within the instructions to isolate a particular group of stitches or where a number of actions are to be performed in one stitch. For example, a shell pattern may be written as (3dc, 1ch, 3dc) all into next sc.

Parentheses are also used where a group of stitches is to be repeated a certain number of times, such as 2dc (1tr, 1ch in next st) 3 times, 1dc, or to give the number of stitches that you should have at the end of a row: (64sts).

Question 161:
Why are some numbers in brackets []?

Numbers in brackets are also used to isolate a group of stitches. Sometimes they are used instead of parentheses, in the same way as above. Occasionally, you may find them used with parentheses in the same line of pattern:

3ch, *(3dc, [4ch, 5dc in 1st of these ch] 3 times, 2dc) 4 times, 1sc, rep from * to end of row.

This means that you begin with 3 turning chains then work 3 double crochet. Make 4 chains and work 5 double crochet into the base of these. Make 4 more chains and 5 double crochet, then 4 more chains and 5 double crochet. So you have 3 rings of double crochet.

Make 2 double crochet. Then start again from the first double crochet within the parentheses and work all the stitches, 4 sets of rings of 5 double crochet separated by 5 double crochet, 3 more times. Next work 1 single crochet. Then start again, working everything after the asterisk, including the 1 single crochet that separates the groups of stitches, until you get to the end of the row.

Question 162:
What does "end last rep" mean?

Some pattern instructions will let you know how many stitches you should have left at the end of a row after working all of the repeats. They will then tell you how to work those last few stitches. For example, 1dc into each of next 4 stitches, *miss 3, 7tr into next, miss 3, 1dc into each of next 7sts; rep from * to last 11sts, miss 3, 7tr into next, miss 3, 1dc into each of last 4sts.

This means you work most of the repeat the same but you end with 4dc instead of 7.

However, some patterns don't give such comprehensive instructions as this. At the end of a line of pattern instructions, you may see the term "end last rep 1dc in last ch, turn."

This means that you continue to work the stitches in the repeats until you come to the end where there will not be enough stitches left to complete it fully. In that case, you work the pattern as far as you can and then check the instructions for how to work the remaining stitches. In the same example as above, the pattern would say:

Rep from *, end last rep 1dc into each of next 4sts, turn.

This would assume that you had worked out that you needed to complete as much as you could of the group first.

BELOW One repeat of pattern plus 11 stitches.

Question 163:
What does "turn" mean?

Where you see the word "turn" at the end of a row or round, it means to turn the work through 180° so the side that was turned away from you now faces you. If you are working back and forth in rows, you are ready to work the next row, working again from right to left until you get to the other end of the row. Some instructions place the turn at the end of a row, followed by the number of turning chains. Some will give the number of turning chains first and then turn at the beginning of the following row. If you are working in the round, you may not always need to turn your work. Make the required number of turning chains and then continue working counterclockwise as before. Sometimes, especially with stitch patterns where you work into spaces, it's easier to turn the work as though it were flat and work your first group of stitches into what was the last space of the round. This method makes it easier to work granny squares as you don't have to slip stitch across any stitches. Just remember which side you have chosen as your wrong side.

BELOW In free-form crochet, sometimes the work is turned and sometimes it is continued with the same side facing.

Question 164:
Can I use old patterns?

The earliest crochet patterns date from the middle of the nineteenth century and did not use standard terms or symbols as they do now. Some were also short on instructions and may not indicate the type of yarn, hook size or gauge. Quite often, a pattern would be written for only one size. It might not include any instructions for shaping, assuming the crocheter would work these out for herself based on a paper pattern that she had made first. Later patterns contained more detail but used a variety of names for the different stitches. Many stitches were referred to as tambour stitches as crochet was possibly derived from this form of work. You may come across terms such as "single tambour," "double tambour" and even "crochet en l'air," meaning crochet without the support of a backing fabric. Also be aware that US terms are different than UK terms. The name of each stitch is one grade lower in America than in most other parts of the world; for instance, a US single crochet is a double crochet elsewhere, a US double crochet is a triple, and so on.

BELOW A selection of early pattern magazines.

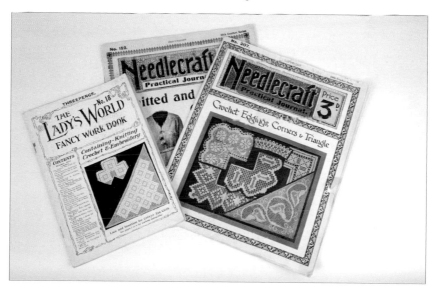

Question 165:
Can I alter a pattern?

Crochet offers great potential for altering and adapting patterns. The simplest change is to work it in a different stitch, providing that the stitch count is the same, that is that you still have a multiple of *x* plus 1. You can also substitute the yarn if you can get the same gauge.

Other ways of altering the pattern include using a smaller hook to get a smaller size. Remember that this will also change the drape of the fabric, making it a little firmer. Conversely, you can use a bigger hook for a larger size, which will make the fabric more open. Obviously, it is an easy matter to alter the length of anything. It is not too difficult to change a sweater to a cardigan or vice versa, or to change a round neck to a turtleneck or scoop neck. Anything more complicated than this will require you to do some math, based on your gauge.

Use a piece of graph paper to work out the existing shape. Then sketch in your variation before working out when and where to place your increases and decreases.

EXPERT TIP

66 Get a friend to help you take accurate body measurements. Wear just your underwear or a close-fitting top. Measure your natural waistline, bust and hips at their fullest parts, length from the top bone at the back of the neck to your waist and length from waist to hip. Also measure the depth of your armhole, the circumference of your upper arm and the width of your back neck.

If you can't get anyone to help you, take the measurements from a sweater that fits you well and you feel comfortable in. Keep a note of these measurements, and check them against the pattern before you start. 99

Question 166:
Can I substitute yarn?

If you are using an old pattern, you will most likely have to substitute the yarn since the one the designer used is probably no longer available. Don't just buy another fingering or worsted weight assuming that it will work the same. The fiber content and even the dye will affect the weight of the yarn. You should always make at least one gauge swatch. If the gauge is given in the pattern you are using, check the

BELOW These yarns are very different and would not work out to the same gauge, even with the same-size hook. Take care to do a big enough sample when using yarns from your stash.

ball band of your substitute yarn to see if it is the same. This is a good indication that the yarn will be suitable. Don't forget to check the length, too, as different fibers can also affect this. Synthetics give you more yards to the gram than wool, which has more length than cotton.

Also try to match the look and feel of the original pattern with the new yarn. If the piece has a soft drape, you would want yours to be the same. Don't pick a heavy cotton yarn when the original was a synthetic one. Consider the finished use of the piece too. A softly spun wool would be no use for a washcloth!

Question 167:
How do I shorten/lengthen a piece of finished crochet?

Lengthening a piece of crochet is simply a matter of joining on yarn at the bottom edge and working either rows of single crochet into the base stitches or working in pattern. If the finished piece is in a patterned stitch, try to match the new section to this. Many crochet stitches look the same upside down. The exception to this are shells and fans, but they will look just as attractive worked the other way. They also look good worked

BELOW Lengthening with a new pattern.

at the bottom edge of a piece of crochet made in one of the plain stitches, such as singles or doubles.

It is possible to shorten crochet from the bottom edge, but this means unpicking each stitch with a tapestry needle. If you need to take off quite a lot, then cut off a few rows first until you get close to your required length. Unpicking from the bound-off edge is easy as it will simply unravel once you have teased out the end that was used to fasten the last stitch.

Question 168:
How can I design my own patterns?

If the starting point is your yarn, play with stitches and hook sizes until you find one you like. Check your gauge. Draw a basic shape, rectangles for back, front, and sleeves, on graph paper using one square for each stitch. If you want something with more shaping – for instance, set-in sleeves and a round neckline – pencil in curves on your graph paper according to your measurements. Then work out from your gauge swatch how many stitches and rows you need to decrease over to achieve these shapes.

Where your inspiration comes from the shape of a piece, make the pattern pieces required to achieve it by using brown paper. Try them against your body. Then look through your crochet books for ideas for stitch and yarn. You don't necessarily need to make a gauge swatch unless you want to try out different hook sizes with your yarn. Make the foundation chain long enough to fit across the width at the bottom of the pattern piece for the back, plus turning chains. Work in your chosen stitch, trying it against the paper pattern as you go. When you reach any shaping, place the crochet against the paper pattern again and count how many stitches to increase or decrease to fit the shape.

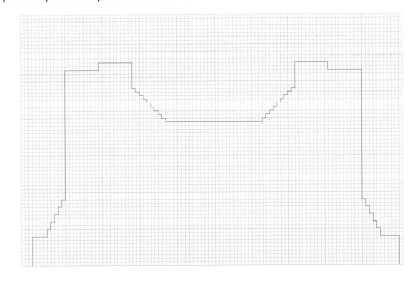

11
OTHER TYPES OF CROCHET

Many variations exist on the basic crochet style – whether differences in the tools you use, the way you use them or what you create by doing so.

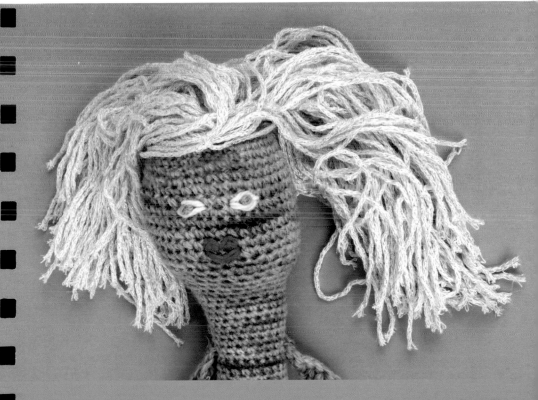

Question 169:
What other types of crochet are there?

As well as the other types of crochet already mentioned in Chapter 9, the majority of which are used to make lace, there are several other variations, some of which require different or additional tools. The main variations are Tunisian crochet, broomstick crochet, hairpin crochet and surface crochet, which are described in more detail later in this chapter. There are also other forms that are worked in just the same way as ordinary crochet but use slightly different techniques, such as crossing stitches or adding beads or other threads, as in aran crochet, beaded crochet and woven crochet. A new variety of crochet is amigurumi, which uses the basic stitches, particularly single crochet, usually worked in the round in spirals.

You may also come across old terms such as sobritto crochet, which refers to the rayon thread that was used for this type of work, or Orvieto and Azores crochet, which are derived from the names of needle laces from those places and are similar to Irish crochet. Net or shadow crochet is similar to filet crochet in appearance but is worked over an existing fabric net or fine muslin. In this respect it is also similar to tambour crochet, described on page 204, which has closer ties to counted thread embroidery than it does to crochet.

Another type of crochet based on needlepoint lace was Maltese crochet, also similar to Irish crochet in that it was made up of leaf shapes joined with short lengths of chain. There were numerous examples of needle laces from different parts of Europe which gave their names to early forms of crochet, names no longer in use, such as Hedebo, Honiton, reticella, Mechlin and torchon. They are all worked using the same stitches as crochet today, but their patterns and appearance were based on the original lace.

Question 170:
What materials do I need for Tunisian crochet?

Tunisian crochet, also known as Afghan or tricot crochet and occasionally shepherd's knitting, is usually used for heavier pieces as the fabric produced is firmer than for ordinary crochet. Because of the way the fabric is produced, holding lots of stitches on the hook and then working them off on the next row, you need a hook long enough to accommodate all of these stitches. It will also need to have a stopper at one end to prevent the stitches

from falling off. The hooks are made from the same kinds of materials as normal hooks. Some of them, especially those longer than 20 inches (50 cm), have flexible cords after a 7 or 8 inch (18 or 20 cm) shaft. Some Tunisian hooks come in sections that can be screwed together to make them even longer. These are ideal for making the ubiquitous Afghan!

Apart from these hooks, all of the other tools are the same as you would use for ordinary crochet: scissors, pins, needles and, obviously, yarn.

BELOW A simple Tunisian crochet hook and an extendable one in three parts.

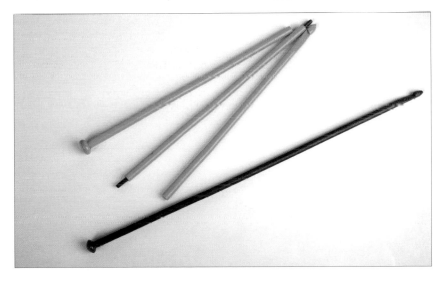

Question 171:
How do I do Tunisian crochet?

The basic Tunisian stitch is known as Tunisian simple stitch or Afghan stitch. Begin with a foundation chain as for ordinary crochet. You don't need to make extra stitches for a turning chain as you do not turn the work. The same side is always facing you in Tunisian crochet. When you have made your chain, work from right to left, and insert your hook into the second chain. Then follow the instructions in the box.

BELOW Tunisian simple stitch, showing some stitches still to be worked off.

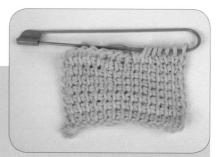

HOW IT'S DONE

1 Yarn over hook and draw it through.

2 Insert your hook into the next chain.

3 Yarn over hook and draw it through.

4 Continue in this way, adding more and more stitches to your hook until you reach the end.

5 The next row is worked by taking the stitches off the hook in pairs.

6 Working from left to right, yarn over hook and draw it through the first loop.

7 Yarn over hook and draw it through two loops.

8 Repeat this last movement to the end of the row.

9 You will now have a piece of fabric that looks a bit like a piece of crochet on its side. There will be a line of vertical bars crossing a line of chains.

10 For the next row, insert your hook from right to left under the second vertical bar.

11 Yarn over hook and draw it through.

12 Insert the hook under the next vertical bar.

13 Yarn over hook and draw it through.

14 Repeat in every bar to the end of the row.

15 On the next row, take off the stitches in pairs again.

Question 172:
What other Tunisian stitches are there?

Other stitches in Tunisian crochet are made by inserting the hook into a different place when you are making all the loops on your hook. A stitch resembling knitting, for example, can be made by inserting the hook from front to back between the vertical loops instead of into them. A purl variation is made by bringing the yarn forward before inserting the hook under the vertical bar, taking the yarn up behind the hook and then drawing a loop through as for Tunisian simple stitch. Another variation is made by working under the chains between the vertical loops. This is known as Tunisian plain stitch.

You can vary all of these alternative stitches by missing vertical bars or by crossing them, that is working the second stitch before the first one across the row. Longer stitches can also be made by wrapping the yarn around the hook and working into the newly made stitch a second time. Working into the stitches of rows lower down also makes interesting pieces, as does working stitches and rows in different colors. Increasing and decreasing can form waves and zigzags as in ordinary crochet. In patterns, the Tunisian simple stitch is abbreviated as tss.

RIGHT Tunisian plain stitch, Tunisian purl and Tunisian simple stitch (from bottom to top).

Question 173:
How do I increase and decrease in Tunisian crochet?

The basic principles of increasing and decreasing in Tunisian crochet are the same as those for ordinary crochet. In Tunisian crochet, though, you usually work the shapings on the row when you are making the stitches and not working them off.

There are two main steps when decreasing: gathering the loops on the hook and then connecting and dropping them off the hook. These are also known as forward and return. This is because when you are working on Tunisian crochet, you are always facing the front of the piece you are making. The forward and return steps ensure that you never need to reverse it.

To decrease, insert the hook under two loops at once, wrap the yarn over and draw it through both loops, making one new stitch. You could also miss one of the vertical bars, but this sometimes leaves a small hole.

Another method of decreasing is to draw the hook through two loops at once on the return row.

At the end of a row, if you need to lose a number of stitches, simply stop before you reach the end and work back. To decrease a number of stitches at the beginning of the row, work a series of slip stitches, pulling the loop of each one through the preceding one, as in binding off.

To increase, after making one stitch through the vertical loop in the normal way, insert the hook under the back loop between this and the next stitch. Wrap the yarn over and draw it through. Then insert the hook under the next vertical loop and make a stitch. Repeat this for however many stitches you need to increase.

As with standard crochet, you can increase and decrease to give a zigzag or wave effect. For example, work the first 2 rows in the normal way. Next pair: *inc 2nd st, work 1tss into each of next 4sts, tss3tog, 1tss into each of next 5sts, inc in next st; rep from * to end. Return. Repeat this pair of rows throughout.

Question 174:
What materials do I need for hairpin crochet?

For hairpin crochet, also known as hairpin lace, you need either an adjustable tool or a set of tools of different sizes, as well as a normal crochet hook.

The hairpins are known as forks or looms and are made from two steel rods, which are inserted into a plastic bar that has holes along its length so that you can vary the width of the rods. Alternatively, the hairpins themselves sometimes come in different widths depending on how wide you want your piece of lace to be and how thick the yarn is.

Hairpin crochet is sometimes erroneously referred to as fork crochet. That is actually another type of hairpin crochet that uses a tool a bit like a short comb but with fewer tines. In both forms of crochet, you also use a crochet hook to draw the yarn through the loops that you have made around the tines. Use a hook that is a little smaller than you would normally use for the yarn weight.

BELOW An adjustable hairpin tool.

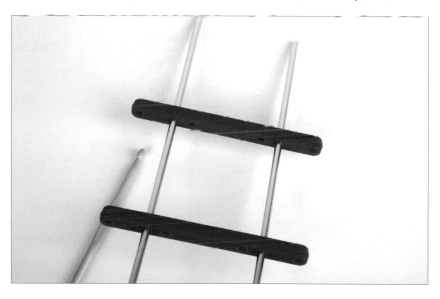

Question 175:
How do I do hairpin crochet?

You begin a piece of hairpin crochet by making a slipknot and putting it onto the right-hand side of the hairpin. Leave the slipknot open. Take the yarn behind the pin and swivel the hairpin clockwise. Insert the crochet hook up through the slipknot, and draw the yarn from the back of the pin through the loop. While keeping your crochet hook in the center of the hairpin, turn the hairpin again, always in the same direction, yarn over hook and draw through the loop. Insert the hook upward into the loop on the left prong, and draw it through so that you have two loops on the hook. Yarn over hook, and draw through the two loops.

Continue like this until you have filled the hairpin with loops. Then slide them off the bottom of the hairpin and continue adding more until the piece is as long as you want it. You can make the central portion wider by working more than one stitch before turning the hairpin. These pieces can then be joined together by linking them with various crochet stitches.

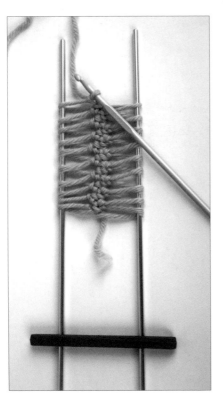

LEFT An adjustable hairpin tool.

Question 176:
How do I do broomstick crochet?

For this technique, you need a dowel or an extra-large knitting needle, about 1 inch (2.5 cm) in diameter, as well as your crochet hook. The additional tool is used to wrap loops of yarn around in order to make very open, lacy stitches.

Begin by making a length of foundation chain with a medium-sized crochet hook. Insert the hook into the first stitch, and draw up a long loop. Holding the stick in your left hand, without twisting it, place the loop just made on its tip. Draw up a loop from the next stitch of your foundation chain, and place this on the stick. Continue in this way until all of the foundation chain stitches have been used. The loops

on the stick are now worked off in various ways, depending on the pattern to be produced.

The simplest pattern is to work a single crochet into each of the loops on the stick. The next row is worked as above, followed by another row of single crochet. You can also work a number of rows of crochet in a pattern of your choice before beginning another row of loops

BELOW A special tool for broomstick crochet.

EXPERT TIP
❝ There is no need to buy special equipment for broomstick crochet. You can use a piece of ordinary broomstick, shaved to a point and sanded down. ❞

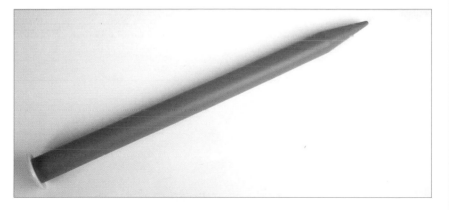

Question 177:
Are there any other broomstick crochet stitches?

A more decorative effect, known as peacock's eye, is achieved if the crochet hook is inserted through several loops at once. Slip four loops from the stick, and twist them once. Make one chain to hold the loops together. Then make four single crochet into the center, or the eye, of this group of four loops. Slip the next four from the stick and do the same. Continue like this to the end of the row when you will have a number of circles joined together.

Do not turn the work for the second row. While working from left to right, draw up a loop from the back loop of each single crochet and place it on the stick. Work the next row to complete the series of eyes as for the first row. Continue in this way for the length required, fastening after a second row.

A variety of patterns can be made by crossing different groups of loops and then working various rows of stitches between the loop rows. These stitches make very quick-to-work afghans and look especially effective in more than one color.

RIGHT Placing the first row of loops on the broomstick (*top*). Taking off the first 4 loops (*middle*). Working single crochet into the loops (*bottom*).

Other Types of Crochet

Question 178:
How do I do surface crochet?

Surface crochet, as its name implies, is worked on a background, which can be an existing fabric or a piece of plain crochet. For a practice piece, make a crochet background of single crochet stitches.

All the stitches in surface crochet are made with the yarn held at the front of the work. You can either work freehand or draw a chart based on the number of stitches in your background. Then follow the chart for the placement of the surface stitches. Make a slipknot on the hook. Then insert the hook down through the fabric and up through the stitch above or alongside it. Make one single crochet. Insert the hook into another stitch, and do the same. You can either keep working single crochet stitches next to each other, clusters or any of the other multiple stitches in various groups. You can also use different colors and form leaf or flower shapes. When you become more experienced, you can work the surface stitches on a more patterned background.

Question 179:
How do I do textured crochet?

Textured crochet is not actually a form of crochet in its own right. It takes techniques from many of the other types of crochet to form pieces that have a textural quality.

Textures are achieved by working into only one of the loops or working around the front or back of the post of the stitch. They can also be made by using any of the multiple stitches such as popcorns, puffs and bobbles or by working stitches into those one or more rows below. This method is most effective when it is worked in more than one color.

Perhaps the most well-known form of textured crochet is Irish crochet, where the multipetal flowers stand raised above the background. Textured motifs such as these are made by working layers of petals behind each other. Detailed instructions for working a traditional rose are given on page 169, but other kinds of flower shapes can be produced by working cups within cups.

Question 180:
What is amigurumi?

Amigurumi is a newly founded Japanese technique for making small dolls, animals and other shapes. *Ami* is the Japanese word for knitting or crochet, and *nuigurumi* means stuffed toy. Because crochet is easier to work in the round than knitting, they are usually made with crochet. Until recently, there were no published patterns for this art form apart from those found on the Internet. With the increase in popularity of these dolls, there are now a few publications coming on the market.

However, these toys are very easy to make once you have learned how to do single crochet in the round. They don't use any complicated stitches, so are suitable for crocheters of all abilities. They are all based on spheres and tubes of various sizes and can be made up as you go along or planned out on paper first. If you don't like the way the shape is turning out, they are easy to undo and begin again. They are intended to be small and cute, so they are also a useful way of using up leftover bits of yarn.

The creatures can be based on real life or be imaginary, for example lips, cakes and other types of food and aliens. There are no published patterns outside Japan, apart from those on the Web; people just make them up as they go along.

Whatever shape they represent, they all have one feature in common. The head or part with the face is much larger in proportion to the rest of the body and limbs. The dolls are worked in the round, in spirals, so it is a good idea to mark the beginning of your round if you want to do any shaping.

Usually they begin with a large ball-shaped head, which is then decreased to make a cylindrical body. However, the head and body can be made separately and joined together. This section is sewn up and stuffed. Sometimes weights, such as those used in beanbags, are added to the base of the body so that the doll does not fall over. Any limbs are crocheted separately, also in the round, and then stitched in place. Additional features can be added with embroidery or pieces of felt.

RIGHT An amigurumi mermaid.

Question 181:
How do I make an amigurumi doll?

For your first attempt, use smooth, light-colored worsted weight yarn and a size G hook. Wrap the yarn once or twice around your finger, and then work a round of single crochet. Join this round with a slip stitch, and pull the tail end of the yarn to close up the hole. Mark your first stitch if you want to do any shaping later. Now continue to work in single crochet around the circle without joining the end of the round to the beginning. Increase on each round as many times as necessary to make the head as large as you want. It is usual to work twice into every stitch of the first round. When the head is the right size, begin to decrease gradually down to the neck, and then continue this number of stitches for the body. Decrease again until you just have a few stitches left. Then thread your yarn through these stitches, and leave a long tail for sewing up after you have stuffed the head and body. Make arms and legs, starting at the hand or foot, in the same way you made the body. Stuff them firmly, draw up the tail end and stitch the limbs to the body. Add any features before or after you do the stuffing, whichever you find easier to do.

After you have made a few practice dolls, use a smaller hook than you would normally use for the weight of yarn so that the stuffing doesn't show through.

Question 182:
How do I do aran crochet?

Aran crochet is worked using the basic crochet stitches but are worked in a form resembling aran knitting. Many of the stitches are raised either by working them around the front or back post or by working them on the surface after you have made a background mesh.

RIGHT Pairs of stitches crossed to form cables.

HOW IT'S DONE

To work a four-stitch cable:

1 Work across to the point where the cable is to be made.

2 Miss 2 stitches and work 1tr around the front posts of the next 2 stitches.

3 Take the hook back over the front of these 2 stitches and work 1tr around the front posts of the 2 stitches that you missed, working them in the correct order.

4 Work the stitches in the normal way on the return row.

5 If you want to work wider cables, you may need to use stitches longer than triples so that they can stretch far enough across the cable.

6 Alternate the cables with groups of bobbles or popcorns to give a more textured aran look. Work stitches resembling moss stitch by alternating half double crochet with single crochet over a number of stitches and rows.

You can also work lines of stitches on the surface, crossing them over and under one another to resemble cables.

Question 183:
How do I do tapestry crochet?

Tapestry crochet is a form of multi-colored crochet using only two colors in a row. The yarn not in use is carried across the back of the work and covered with the working yarn as you go. The designs are almost always worked in single crochet. Because of this, they are geometric or stylized pictorial forms based on squares, as in counted-thread embroidery. Cross-stitch and other square-based designs can be easily transposed to tapestry crochet because it can be worked in rows or in rounds.

The designs are quicker to work if you learn to carry more than one color in your hand at a time. Work a few stitches with the main yarn, crocheting over the contrast yarn to hold it in place. Switch to the contrast yarn, and carry the main yarn along the top of the stitches that are to be worked in contrast. Join the colors in the usual way, by working as far as the last two loops in the first color and then using the second color for the last move. Work in single crochet in the normal way, but cover the strand of main yarn at the same time.

Question 184:
How do I do woven crochet?

Woven crochet is maybe the simplest form of crochet. The only difficult part is in planning your design. First of all, you work a background mesh, which can be all one color or a series of stripes. The mesh is usually made in the same way as filet crochet, with a single or double crochet stitch followed by one or two chains. The more chains separating the stitches, the more strands you need to weave through each column of spaces. When the mesh is finished, cut strands of yarn to the appropriate length and weave them in and out of the spaces. By changing colors across the columns, you can make a tartan effect afghan. You can make a mesh with pattern stitches, and clusters or popcorns are very effective. Instead of weaving strands of yarn through the spaces, you could also use I-cord, crochet cord, ribbon or strips of fabric. They can be woven in any direction and produce a completely reversible fabric. Finish the edges with two or three rows of single crochet, or leave the ends loose to act as a fringe.

BELOW Background mesh woven with crochet chains or with strands of yarn.

Question 185:
How do I do tambour crochet?

Tambour crochet is related to embroidery as it is worked onto a piece of fabric, fine linen, muslin or cotton lawn, which is held in a doubled hoop or tambour. It does not form a fabric in its own right but is used for decoration. The finished result looks like embroidered chain stitch but is quicker to produce with a crochet hook, especially if you use a free-standing hoop that will allow you to use both hands.

BELOW A hoop suitable for tambour crochet work.

Hold the crochet hook above the work and the thread below it. Push the hook down through the fabric, and catch the thread below. Draw the thread up through the fabric.

With the loop still on the hook, insert it again a short distance away and draw up another loop. Draw this second loop though the first one as if creating a slip stitch. Continue inserting the hook through the fabric and drawing each new loop through the one already on the hook.

The stitches made in this way should all be the same size.

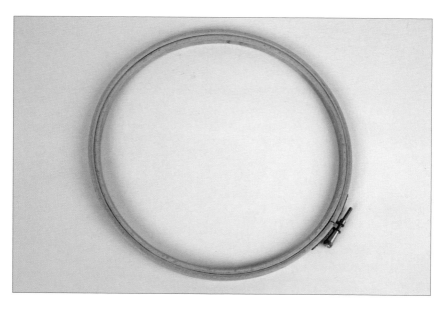

Question 186:
How do I do beaded crochet?

Anything with a hole in it can be added to crochet, either as you go along or after you have finished the work. The design is usually worked from a chart, showing the placement of the beads, or you can add them at random. To add beads as you go, first you need to thread them onto your yarn in the reverse order, that is, the ones intended for the last row should go onto the yarn first. They will fall to the opposite side of the piece to the one that is facing you, so remember to apply them on the wrong-side rows.

The simplest method of attaching beads is to work as far as the position of the bead and then slide it down the yarn until it rests against the last stitch. Insert the hook in the next stitch, and draw through the yarn.

Yarn over hook, and draw through the two loops. This fastens the bead in place. Continue adding beads in this way according to the chart. You can add them to every stitch or work a few stitches in between. You can also add them on every row.

If you have started your work and then decide that you want to add beads later, you can use a hook small enough to pass through the hole in the bead and bring the yarn back through the hole before completing the stitch in the normal way. This is a useful technique for adding beads on the last row of an edging. Alternatively, you can stitch them on using a matching fine thread.

BELOW Suitable beads for small crochet pieces.

12
FINISHING TOUCHES

Complete your pieces of crochet work with your choice of
the many possible finishing touches, from buttons and pockets
to tassels and fringes.

Question 187:
How do I block a piece of crochet?

Blocking means to shape the piece of crochet to the measurements as given in the pattern instructions. If you have several separate pieces that need to be joined together, block them individually before joining the seams. It is easier to match them together accurately then.

Check the ball band of the yarn before you start to block, making sure the yarn can be wet. If so, pin the pieces on a cloth-covered board to the correct measurements. Then spray it all over with tepid water and leave it to dry. Alternatively, you can cover it with very damp towels. Remember to use rustproof pins if you choose this method.

If the ball band says dry clean only, pin it out as above. With an iron set to a low heat, gently press the fabric, lifting the iron before moving to the next area. Some fibers, such as cotton and linen, benefit from a steam press, which is the same as above but with the iron set to steam. If you have very textured stitches, hold the iron a little above the fabric, hovering it across the work. Again, leave it to dry before removing the piece from the board.

BELOW Pinning out a piece of scalloped crochet before pressing.

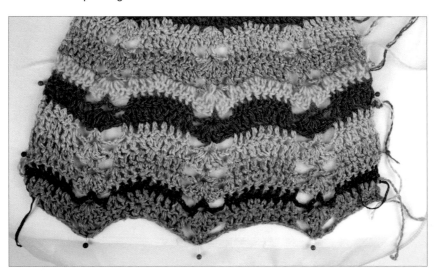

Question 188:
How do I join the pieces?

There are various ways of joining garment pieces together. When you have blocked the pieces, place them together with right sides facing each other and backstitch through the stitches either at the edge, if the yarn is bulky, or one stitch in from the edge if it is not.

Alternatively, you can crochet them together. To do this, place right sides facing each other and work a row of slip stitch or single crochet through both thicknesses of fabric. You could also work the crochet stitches on the right side of the fabric for a decorative trim.

Another method that can be especially useful for bulky yarns is a woven seam. Lay the pieces with the seams to be joined side by side with wrong sides facing up. With matching yarn a little finer than that used for the crochet, begin at the top of the seam. Join the yarn firmly to the top. Then take it around the post of the first stitch, over to the other piece and around the post of its first stitch. Continue in this way, weaving back and forth around the posts of each stitch. Then pull on it gently to close the seam.

BELOW Joining two pieces of crochet together.

Question 189:
How do I make buttonholes?

Horizontal buttonholes are easiest to make in single crochet. Work a number of stitches until you come to the location of your first buttonhole. Skip however many stitches it will take to accommodate your button, and work that number of chains in their place. Then continue in single crochet to the next buttonhole. If you are working longer stitches than single crochet, remember to allow for their height when deciding how many stitches to skip.

Vertical buttonholes are worked in two stages. When you reach the required point, work three or four stitches. Then turn and work a few rows over only these stitches. Work enough rows to fit the size of your button and then fasten the yarn. Rejoin it to the stitch at the point where you turned or one stitch away for a large button. Work the same number of rows as for the first section. On the next row, work back along the first few stitches to complete the buttonhole.

A third way of making buttonholes, which is useful when you have forgotten to make them, is to work button loops. Work in single crochet along the edge of the band. At the point where you want the button, make a chain long enough to fit it. Turn and slip stitch the chain to a stitch three or four stitches away, or however many stitches it will take to fit the button. Work one single crochet for each chain into the loop. Then continue across the row in single crochet to the next button loop.

RIGHT A buttonhole worked on the edge.

Question 190:
How do I make buttons?

If you can't find suitable buttons for your crochet, you can make your own. To make a Dorset button, you need a small metal or plastic ring. Work over the edge of the ring with single crochet stitches. Join with a slip stitch to the first stitch, and fold the outside edges of the stitches into the center. Break off the yarn, leaving a long end. Thread this end into a needle. Then make spokes across the center of the ring by taking the yarn diagonally across to each of the stitches in turn. This should fill the center of the ring. It can be decorated with beads or embroidery stitches if you wish.

A ball button is made by first working a row of single crochet into a circle of yarn. Next, work another round, increasing in every stitch.

For a larger button, work another round, increasing in every alternate stitch. Continue in this way as if making a circle. When the button is the width you want, work decreases at the same rate as your increases until you have only a few stitches left. Break off the yarn. Thread it through the edge of these stitches, drawing up the yarn tightly. Stuff the center of the ball with some spare yarn. Then draw up the tail end from the beginning and fasten it firmly into the ball or use it to sew the button onto the garment.

RIGHT A ball button.

BELOW Dorset buttons.

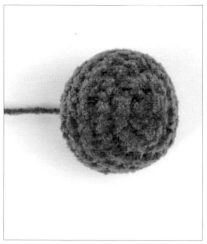

Question 191:
How do I pick up stitches around a shaped edge?

If you are working an edging around an inner curve, such as a neckline or an armhole, it will look neatest if you work with a hook one or two sizes smaller than for the main piece. At a round neckline, for example, work one single crochet into the head of each stitch at the back neck. Then work one or two stitches into the side of each stitch down the left front neck edge. The number you work into each stitch will depend on how tall the stitches of the main piece are. Single crochet will only take one, and double crochet will need two. When you reach the curved part of the neckline, work one stitch into each row unless the stitches are very long, where you will probably need two. Work one stitch into each stitch across the front of the neck, and then work the right front neck edge to match. Work into the sides of the stitches rather than between them to avoid holes.

When you are working around an outer curve, again use a smaller hook. This time, increase the occasional stitch by working twice into one around the sharpest edge of the curve.

BELOW Stitches picked up around a straight edge.

Question 192:
How do I add pockets?

The simplest pockets are added after the work is completed. Make two pieces, one for each pocket, then tack them in place and stitch them by oversewing. Use the same yarn or a closely matching finer one if you have used bulky yarn for the main piece.

Simple pockets can be set into the side seams of a jacket. You can either work them as part of the back, making little flaps that stick out sideways, or you can add them afterward. If you add them afterward, you can make them in a finer yarn, avoiding some of the bulk that you get with these kinds of pockets. Work several single crochet along the side seam of the back, and then continue in rows for as deep as you want the pockets to be. Fasten and stitch the pocket flaps to the corresponding position on the fronts of the garment. Add a shallow edging along the front opening if you want.

The other kind of pockets are those that are worked before you begin the fronts. When you reach the point on the front where the top of the pocket will be, crochet across the stitches of the pocket lining, miss the same number of stitches on the front, and then crochet to the end. Again, you can work an edging along the front opening and then stitch the pocket to the wrong side of the garment by oversewing.

EXPERT TIP

❝ Because crochet won't unravel when you cut the yarn, another kind of pocket can be made when the work is finished, an afterthought pocket. Mark the line of stitches where you want the pocket to be, then cut the yarn at the center and gradually unpick the stitches across the row. Join new yarn to one corner, and work 1 single crochet into each of the loops left hanging. Work the pocket downward, and fasten when it is big enough. Rejoin the yarn to what will be the front opening, and work two rows of single crochet or one single crochet and one crab stitch across the other set of live stitches. ❞

Question 193:
How do I make crochet cord?

A length of foundation chain makes the simplest crochet cord. However, it is not very strong, and it can cut into your hands if you are using it as a bag handle. For a thicker cord, work a row of slip stitch along the chain. To make it thicker again, work another row back down the other side of the chain.

A softer chain is made by working single crochet into each stitch of the foundation chain, and then, to make it thicker, work one chain and a single crochet into each stitch along the other side. More and more rows of single crochet can be added in this way, remembering to work three stitches into each of the stitches at the corners.

If you are not sure how long you will want your cord to be, then you can work it lengthwise over three or four stitches, in single or double crochet. For tapered ends, begin with three chains, work three or four double crochet into the first one, continue for the length required, and then work the last row as a decrease over all the stitches.

Other cords are made by following the instructions for the different foundation chains.

BELOW An example of crochet cord.

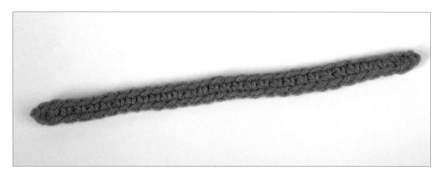

Question 194:
How do I make a fringe?

Fringes make an attractive finish to a scarf or shawl. They are simple to work but take more yarn than you would expect. So remember to allow for this when deciding to add fringe to a pattern that is not trimmed in this way.

To make a fringe, cut enough lengths of yarn to fit across your scarf. If you had 40 stitches in the scarf, you will probably want a fringe attached to every alternate one, so you need 20 times however many strands you want in each fringe.

Make the lengths long enough to be worthwhile — at least 12 inches (25 cm) is necessary to make a nice, full fringe. Gather together the required amount of strands, and fold them in half to form a loop. Insert your hook from front to back through the edge of your crochet, and grasp the loop of fringe. Pull it back through the stitch. With the loop still on the hook, grasp the doubled strands and pull them through the loop. Trim the fringe afterward so that all of the tassels are the same length. If you make very long fringes, you can tie them together in pairs for a different look.

A separate fringe edging that can be removed for washing can be made by working a number of chains, such as 6, *work 1sc into each stitch, then work 50ch, fold these back in half and work into the 6sc again. Rep from * from * until the fringe is the length required.

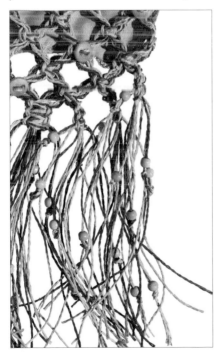

LEFT A fringe on the edge of a completed crochet scarf.

Question 195:
How do I make spiral tassels?

Another way of trimming crochet is to make spirals, or curlicues. They are made individually and then sewn to the fabric afterward.

Begin with a foundation chain of about 30 stitches. Use a large hook because you are going to be working a number of increases into each of these stitches. Change to a smaller hook, and work three double crochet into the fourth chain, then four double crochet into every chain to the end. The work will gradually begin to twist, and you may find it difficult to work into the later stitches. Fasten off the yarn at the end, leaving a tail for sewing the

spiral on to the main fabric. You can make longer spirals by working more foundation chain at the beginning. You can make wider ones by working more rows, increasing in every stitch as before.

You can trim a scarf or shawl with spiral tassels, or you can trim it with small balls made in the same way as ball buttons described on page 211. You can instead make chain loops with beads added to them.

BELOW A spiral tassle, or curlicue.

Question 196:
How do I wash crochet?

Crochet is heavier than knitting; it takes approximately a third more yarn for the same-size item than knitting does. Although you wash it in the same way as knitting, by following the instructions on the ball band and not changing the temperature of the rinsing water, you need to be extra careful in drying it. If the ball band says it is safe to tumble dry, then it should be. Because crochet stretches when it is hung up, even when it is dry, always lay it flat. When it is completely dry, store it neatly folded in a drawer or on a shelf. If it won't be used for some time, place tissue, preferably acid free, between the folds. To keep white cotton items sparkling white, wrap them in blue tissue paper. Store items away from direct light and excessive humidity. Make sure that they are clean and dry when you put them away.

If you are not sure of the fiber content, hold a lighted flame to one end of an extra piece of yarn. If it melts, it is synthetic. If it only singes, it is wool and will probably need to be hand washed or dry-cleaned.

BELOW Wrapping a piece of crochet in tissue.

Question 197:
How do I stiffen crochet?

Some decorative crochet items look much better if they are stiffened. You can also shape stiffened crochet pieces into bowls and baskets or even more ornate pieces.

For cloths and doilies that don't need to be shaped into three dimensions, use a commercial starch, in spray form, a liquid or a powder. Wash the piece first, and then immerse it into the starch solution. Leave it to soak for two or three minutes, then remove it and block it on a clean towel to soak up any surplus solution. Leave it to dry away from direct light.

For three-dimensional objects, you need something that will be more permanent. You can use various mixtures. In all cases, wash your piece first and let it dry. Boil equal amounts of sugar and water together to make a thin syrup. Leave it to cool. Then immerse the piece of crochet in the solution, making sure that it has all been coated. Squeeze out any excess moisture, and leave it to dry naturally over a mold of the appropriate shape. If you can't find a suitable mold, make something out of plastic bags stuffed with cotton balls or old pantyhose. For small items such as Christmas tree ornaments, window decorations, etc., pin out the piece onto paper, using rustproof pins, and spray with hairspray or spray starch. This method gives only a temporary stiffness. You may need to repeat it if the piece is to be hanging for several days. You could also use equal parts of glue and water or purchase various commercial products.

EXPERT TIP

66 **If the piece is too stiff, hold it over some steam to soften it slightly, then reshape it and allow it to dry again.** 99

Question 198:
Can I felt crochet?

The main thing to remember when felting crochet is that it is more likely to shrink in length than in width, so be sure to make it extra long rather than extra wide. Stitches that are longer than double crochet will shrink more than those made with single crochet. The fibers will also stick together. So if you are making

something that has a back and front, put a plastic bag between the two pieces.

The best results are obtained with 100% wool, but it is worth trying other animal products such as alpaca and mohair. Make your item, then put it into the washing machine with something like a pair of jeans (make sure that the color won't run!) and wash in hot water. It will probably take about 15 minutes, but the actual timing depends on the machine and the stitches you have used. Longer stitches take longer.

You can also felt by hand, using hot water and dish liquid. Pound the crochet in this mixture, using your hands in the same way as you would when making dough. The more you agitate it, the better it will felt. Rinse it in some cold water, and then return it to the hot liquid and pound it again. Repeat this process until it is as felted as you want it. Squeeze out the excess moisture, and leave it to dry.

LEFT A felted bag.

Question 199:
How do I look after my hooks?

Hooks can easily become damaged, either through normal use, especially if you crochet with wire, or by being stored incorrectly. Don't stand them point down in a can or jar, and don't just throw them haphazardly into a box with your other needlework tools. Keep them in their individual plastic sleeves or store them together in a specially made case.

Clean them from time to time with a cloth soaked in methylated spirit to remove any grease that has been transferred from your hands.

If you use wooden hooks, you may find that they flake after a while and begin to snag the yarn. Rub them down with some very fine sandpaper, and then polish them with wood oil or beeswax. Plastic hooks can be washed in soapy water and dried on a soft cloth. Bone or ivory hooks can be cleaned with a cloth that is just slightly damp. Never immerse them in water as they can warp.

Below Don't store your hooks head down in a jar. Keep them in their packets.

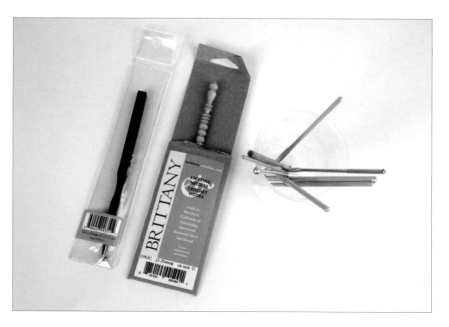

Question 200:
How do I care for antique crochet?

If your crochet is already clean, wrap it in acid-free tissue paper and store it flat or rolled over a cardboard cylinder if too large to store flat. It must have good air circulation, so keep it in your living space rather than in the cellar or attic. The main causes of damage to any textiles are light, excessive heat, dampness and insects.

At least once a year, take the crochet out of its wrapping and air it. At the same time, inspect it for moth or mildew damage. If you find any, isolate it from other pieces immediately. If it is dusty, cover it with a piece of net and vacuum it lightly before refolding it along different lines and putting it back in the tissue paper. Keep it somewhere cool, dry and dark.

If you find that it's a bit dirty but not stained, wash it in mild soap with no chemical additives or bleaching products. Rinse it in cool water, and then place it flat on a clean towel. Block it to shape, pin it with rustproof pins and then leave it to dry naturally. If it is too big to pin you can cover it with a white cloth and press it while it is still damp using the iron on its coolest setting.

If the crochet is very stained, you will have to decide whether it is worth the risk of trying to get the stains out. There are various ways of doing it, but some are a little drastic. First dampen the stained part. Then try squeezing lemon juice onto it and leaving the piece to dry in the sun. A sprinkling of salt sometimes helps Another method is to soak the stain in a solution of washing soda or a weak solution of dishwasher powder or liquid. There are also commercial preparations that you can use.

EXPERT TIP

66 **Do not starch cotton that is going to be stored for some time. Although cotton is not vulnerable to attack by moths, the starch can be an attractant as a food source.** 99

Useful Information

Table of international crochet symbols

	Stitch symbol
	⌒
slip stitch	●
single crochet	x or + or |
half double crochet	T
double crochet	Ŧ
triple crochet	₮
double triple crochet	₮
triple triple crochet	₮
front post double crochet	ʒ
back post double crochet	ɛ
x-stitch	X
3-chain picot	▽
2-single crochet decrease	⋀
2-single crochet increase	⋁
puff stitch	⬧
popcorn	⬤
loop stitch	⊎

Abbreviations

app	approximately
beg	beginning, begin
bet	between
bk lp or bl	back loop
blo	back loop only
bp	back post
bpdc	back post double crochet
bpsc	back post single crochet
bptr	back post triple crochet
ch	chain stitch
ch-sp	chain space
cl	cluster
cont	continue
dc	double crochet
dc2tog	double crochet two stitches together
dec	decrease
dtr	double triple
fl or ft lp	front loop
flo	front loop only
foll	follow, following
fp	front post
fpdc	front post double crochet
fpsc	front post single crochet
fptc	front post triple crochet
hdc	half double crochet
hk	hook
inc	increase
lc	left cross
lp(s)	loop(s)

m	marker
m1	make one
p	picot
pat(s)	pattern(s)
pc	popcorn
pm	place marker
prev	previous
rc	right cross
rem	remain(ing)
rep	repeat
rnd(s)	rounds
rs	right side
rev sc	reverse single crochet
sc	single crochet

sc2tog	single crochet 2 stitches together
sk	skip
sl	slip
sl st	slip stitch
sp(s)	space(s)
st(s)	stitch(es)
tbl	through back loop
tch or tc	turning chain
together	together
tr	triple crochet
tr tr	triple triple crochet
ws	wrong side
yo	yarn over
yoh	yarn over hook

Hook sizes for aluminium, wood & plastic hooks

US size	Metric size	Old UK size
B-1	2½	12
C-2	3	11
D-3	3¼	10
E-4	3½ or 3¾	9
F-5	4	8
G-6	4¼ or 4½	7
H-8	5	6
I-9	5½	5
J-10	6	4
K-10½	7	3
L-11	8	2
M-13	9	1
N-15	10	0
P-16	15	-
Q	16	-
S	19	-

Hook sizes for steel hooks

US size	Metric size	Old UK size
00	3.5	-
0	3.25	0
1	2.75	1
2	2.25	1½
3	2.1	2
4	2.0	2½
5	1.9	3
6	1.8	3½
7	1.65	4
8	1.5	4½
9	1.4	5
10	1.3	5½
11	1.1	6
12	1.0	6½
13	0.85	7
14	0.75	-

Index